SYLVIA BROWNE'S
LESSONS FOR LIFE

ALSO BY SYLVIA BROWNE

BOOKS/CARD DECK

Adventures of a Psychic (with Antoinette May)
Astrology Through a Psychic's Eyes
Blessings from the Other Side (with Lindsay Harrison)
Contacting Your Spirit Guide (book-with-CD)
Conversations with the Other Side
Heart and Soul card deck
A Journal of Love and Healing (with Nancy Dufresne)
Life on the Other Side (with Lindsay Harrison)
Meditations
Mother God
The Other Side and Back (with Lindsay Harrison)
Past Lives, Future Healing (with Lindsay Harrison)
Prayers
Secrets & Mysteries of the World
Sylvia Browne's Book of Angels
Sylvia Browne's Book of Dreams (with Lindsay Harrison)
Visits from the Afterlife (with Lindsay Harrison)

The Journey of the Soul Series
(available individually or in a boxed set)

God, Creation, and Tools for Life (Book 1)
Soul's Perfection (Book 2)
The Nature of Good and Evil (Book 3)

AUDIO/CD PROGRAMS

Angels and Spirit Guides
Healing Your Body, Mind, and Soul
Life on the Other Side (audio book)
Making Contact with the Other Side
Meditations
The Other Side of Life
Prayers
Secrets & Mysteries of the World
Sylvia Browne's Book of Angels (audio book)
Sylvia Browne's Tools for Life
and . . .
The Sylvia Browne Newsletter (bimonthly)

All of the above are available at your local bookstore, or may be ordered by visiting: Hay House USA: **www.hayhouse.com;** Hay House Australia: **www.hayhouse.com.au;** Hay House UK: **www.hayhouse.co.uk;** Hay House South Africa: **orders@psdprom.co.za**

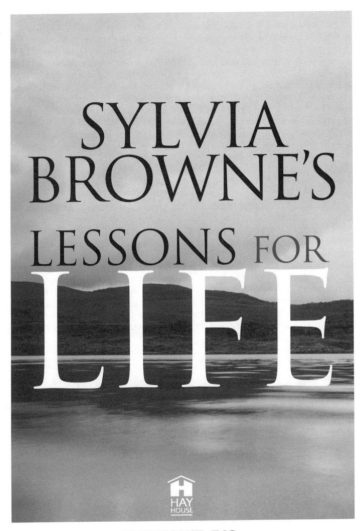

SYLVIA BROWNE'S
BROWNE'S
LESSONS FOR
LIFE

HAY HOUSE, INC.
Carlsbad, California
London • Sydney • Johannesburg
Vancouver • Hong Kong

Published and distributed in the United States by: Hay House, Inc., P.O. Box 5100, Carlsbad, CA 92018-5100 • *Phone:* (760) 431-7695 or (800) 654-5126 • *Fax:* (760) 431-6948 or (800) 650-5115 • www.hayhouse.com • *Published and distributed in Australia by:* Hay House Australia Pty. Ltd., 18/36 Ralph St., Alexandria NSW 2015 • *Phone:* 612-9669-4299 • *Fax:* 612-9669-4144 • www.hayhouse.com.au • *Published and distributed in the United Kingdom by:* Hay House UK, Ltd. • Unit 62, Canalot Studios • 222 Kensal Rd., London W10 5BN • *Phone:* 44-20-8962-1230 • *Fax:* 44-20-8962-1239 • www.hayhouse.co.uk • *Published and distributed in the Republic of South Africa by:* Hay House SA (Pty), Ltd., P.O. Box 990, Witkoppen 2068 • *Phone/Fax:* 27-11-706-6612 • orders@psdprom.co.za • *Distributed in Canada by:* Raincoast • 9050 Shaughnessy St., Vancouver, B.C. V6P 6E5 • *Phone:* (604) 323-7100 • *Fax:* (604) 323-2600

Editorial supervision: Jill Kramer • *Design:* Amy Rose Szalkiewicz

Library of Congress Cataloging-in-Publication Data

Browne, Sylvia.
 Sylvia Browne's lessons for life / Sylvia Browne.
  p. cm.
 ISBN 1-4019-0087-9 (pbk.)
 1. Spiritual life—Miscellanea. I. Title.
 BF1999.B7155 2004
 131—dc21

                      2002155118

             ISBN 13: 978-1-4019-0087-8
             ISBN 10: 1-4019-0087-9

          08 07 06 05   7 6 5 4
          1st printing, October 2004
          4th printing, February 2005

     Printed in the United States of America

For my children, my friends, and my ministers.

CONTENTS

AUTHOR'S NOTE

It's been said that each journey starts with a single step. The book you hold in your hands happens to be an eight-step program

that will live in your heart and not only make you feel better, but will hopefully help you assist others in finding their ordained path, too. This path is easier than you think . . . once you get rid of all the behavioral overlays that keep your soul from breathing and flying free. Through these eight weeklong steps toward the soul's perfection, you'll explore why you came here and why you must resolve to seek good and stay on track. This, in turn, will bring you joy and fulfillment—as well as a release of stress.

When you put your all into this program and complete it, you'll come out feeling refreshed, renewed, and released from your doubts, fears, and phobias. You will, through your own introspection, become more spiritual, which naturally leads to being more psychic. You'll know that life is just a textbook of learning played out on the stage of this world, and when it's over, you'll exit behind the curtains and go Home from whence you came.

By completing just one step each week—reading the information at the beginning of the week, repeating the meditation and affirmation daily, and completing the exercises throughout the seven days— you'll come away with a depth of understanding that will not only help you, but will also pique your soul to search for more. In this intense, honest examination of your life—during which you'll uncover answers from your deepest truth center—you'll not only recognize patterns of unwanted guilt, you'll also discover which lessons you came here to learn and why you picked them. Additionally, you'll see what you needlessly hold on to, whether it be people, places, or things. Then you'll come to the realization through truth, not just blind faith, that although loved ones come in and out of your life, it's all for the gigantic plan of increasing your soul's capability for learning—for yourself and for God.

This book will help you find almost every facet you need to help you arrive at your own spirituality, and it will help you get over your feelings of guilt, loss, and instability. The information within will answer questions in more depth than I've previously explored or written about, and the meditations and exercises will enhance your consciousness to bring you closer to your divine purpose and your ultimate love affair with God.

This journey will stay with you and change you from victim to victor—empowering you to meet your goals and overcome all darkness that comes your way. You'll leave behind all those behavioral overlays that you've collected to protect yourself, and decide not to let anyone or anything throw you back into a negative pattern again. You'll be reborn into your own spirituality and the great celebration of your own unique, immortal soul, which is loved and cherished by God.

Put all you have into this, and you'll get a hundredfold back. Good luck!

STEP 1

HOW TO REALIZE YOUR OWN ESSENCE AND WHAT THAT CONSISTS OF IN A SPIRITUAL SENSE

Aristotle said it better than anyone: "The soul is the cause or source of the living body." We can go through all the large and small facets of our personality—our likes and dislikes; our thoughts, temperaments, pet peeves, irritations; even our hates and loves—but we have to decipher the true essence of our soul and separate that from what comes with this human life, and all its perfections and failings. The soul in its ultimate purest form has one innate purpose, and that is to perfect and learn for God.

The purpose of this first step is not only to find your essence, but to get rid of the erroneous behavioral overlays that keep your soul from soaring. If you can free yourself of needless guilt; stop determining who you are based on other people's opinions; overcome unwanted criticism; keep time to your own drum (whatever the beat may be); and live by your sense of what's right, which is innate in your own good, unique soul, then you've taken a giant step toward the perfection of your own essence.

What If I'm a Bad Person?

People are always asking me, "Why don't I have a better opinion of myself?" "Why do I feel off track?" and "Am I a bad person?"

In the first place, on a really logical note, bad people, or those who are off track, don't *care* and would never ask these questions. They seem unconcerned with such thoughts and are truly convinced that they're justified in whatever action they take . . . wrong or right. Good people are always more subject to guilt and worry. Why, you may ask? Easy— because good souls monitor themselves and have a built-in alarm system that keeps them on track.

Part of that built-in system is called *guilt.* This is a mechanism that keeps us (or should keep us) from doing harm to another person, animal, place, or thing. It's also been called *the conscience,* and it's the message that's written on the soul, the one that Jesus brought to the foreground: "Do unto others as you would have them do unto you."

Yet I've noticed, during my 49 years of being a professional psychic as well as a humanitarian, that people often take on guilt for reasons beyond their control. For instance, a mother who has done everything humanly possible to love and nurture her children will have one kid who turns out badly, and then she'll go and blame herself. She might never think to look past the fact that this entity picked his or her life to learn how to experience adversity, while she, the mother, chose her chart to learn patience and tolerance. There's too much in life that we take on and own when it isn't ours to absorb. (Now if the mother had made a concerted effort with malice, forethought, and motive to create a bad child, then guilt should be a reality. . . .)

The people who don't make it to the bedside of a dying friend or relative usually feel guilt, too. But these folks need to seriously ask themselves if they did this out of mean-spirited contrivance. Did they deliberately not make it in time? Of course not!

This also applies to all the other actions we could list, from the small and insignificant to the larger and more important.

I remember one time when my grandson, William, was playing in the backyard at his sister's birthday party and he collided with another little boy, breaking his own leg. For a few minutes, I went through that old, programmed tape: "Why hadn't I been closer? Why didn't I see it coming?" (After all, as I've said many times before, I'm psychic, but not about myself or my family.) Then I had to shake it off. Would I have prevented it if I could? For God's sake, yes! Was I meant to? No— this was part of my grandson's chart. Later William said, "I guess I have to look where I'm going and be more careful." Lesson learned, so why should I put myself through those feelings in a situation I had no control over? Besides, if I did, I'd just be interfering with the learning process.

I've found that just about all of us have done something on the spur of the moment, or in an emotional outburst, that we're sorry for (and we should be), so we try to make amends. But to obsess your entire life over what can't be changed puts a block on your soul and mars the essence of your true self—especially when a simple "I'm sorry" would have been sufficient.

What Makes Us Who We Are?

We've been raised on guilt and the expectations of others to such an extent that sometimes we feel as if we don't even know who we really are. We may even forget about free will and act in ways that correspond with what others have chosen for us. So much of our life falls into this pit of *determinism,* a term used to explain what happens when we let other people select our identities for us. This is a phenomenon that works on a small scale as well as a large one, and it operates on the physical, emotional, and even a soul level.

Let's begin by looking at determinism in very simplistic terms. Imagine that when you were young, someone told you that you looked great in red. Like it or not, at an unguarded moment, it goes into your consciousness, and now forever after you think you look fantastic in this color. Forget the fact that like me, red may make you look as if you have a nasty case of rosacea. (My sister, bless her heart, wore a bubble cut in high school and everyone told her it looked great. Now, at age 60, it's not so cute . . . but if it makes her happy, who cares?)

There are other deeper determinism factors that can almost wreck our self-worth. Again, from my own experience, when I was 16, I overheard my mother say to someone on the telephone, "Well, Sharon [my sister] is the real beauty, but Sylvia has personality." Of course as a teenager, I couldn't have cared less about personality—I wanted to be the beauty! If I'd let that seep in too deep, it might have had a negative result, but I finally decided, "Well if that's what it is, I'll just be my own person."

Dig deeply into your memories of this life to see what, when, where, and how your negative self-definitions were planted—and who planted them. Really mull it over. Chances are you'll realize that it's the unguarded moments in which someone can come up with a zinger that hurts, and you accept it as part of your own identity: "You're overly sensitive," "You're shaped like a pear," or my personal favorite, "You're too honest." The list is endless.

Say you work for a miserable, critical boss who always puts you down. Before long, you might start looking at yourself through this person's eyes, and "own" the fact that you're inept, stupid, or whatever. I've also seen this in friendships and even, sadly, marriages. Of course the person who's giving out insults always has the fallback position of making you feel inadequate by saying, "Well, I guess you can't take criticism." In a word, no! I'm a firm believer in the absolute truth that there isn't any criticism that's constructive. In my opinion, it's all destructive. The very word *criticism* is negative. There are many ways to approach a situation with tact, not with a derogatory comment.

Remember that this kind of judgment stems from other people's insecurities, and when you find yourself surrounded by critical people, you must leave. And when you do, face the fact that you weren't inept or stupid before this, so why would you believe you are now?

Sometimes this is easier said than done. For some reason, the negative tends to stick and the positive dims. That's because this world is a negative environment, and such energy flourishes here. It's like my spirit guide Francine says, "When the soul comes into a human form, it becomes vulnerable."

To counter negative determinism, reflect on the positive ideas about yourself that you absorbed from others. Adopting these definitions is your right, because whatever you "collect" determines what you are. Gather these positive sayings from your memory banks and focus on them, and then take those hurtful messages and put them out of your mind.

Moving On

The other concept that can put a crimp in our soul's essence is that elusive concept of *forgiveness.* We've grown up with people telling us that to forgive is divine, and I wholeheartedly believe this. The only problem is, we aren't divine! We're still in the process of learning and finding the divinity of our soul. Do I believe in forgiveness? Sure I do, but I also know that there are certain events that are truly impossible for some of us to forgive.

A reporter once asked the mother of a boy who was brutally murdered if she forgave her son's killer. That mother looked the journalist square in the eye and said, "No, but I've given it to God, because it's too much for me." I thought, *Good for you!* We spend too much time trying to forgive when we can't, rather than just letting it go and giving it to God.

Of course, sometimes you have to work through the animosity and even feelings of vengeance before you can get to that place of releasing it to God and the universe. I've even said at lectures, "There are some people (just a few) I enjoy hating," because there's nothing wrong with hating evil. Why in God's name should we embrace it, love it, and forgive it? Our Lord certainly was very candid when he said, "Don't cast your pearls before swine," and "Shake the dust off your feet [and walk away]." In other words, move on—what goes around comes around, and everything will even out in the end.

In the essence of the soul, there's a built-in *karma,* which, by the way, means "soul's experience." Now don't confuse what I'm saying here with the idea that everything you do—again, without malice aforethought—has to show up in a future life (or even in this life). I've been places where *everything* you say or do is a no-no, because you'll get bad karma. I find it amazing that we've tried so hard to dispel a vengeful God who sends us to "hell," only to substitute karma that never ends, on a wheel where "you hit me and I hit you" for eternity. Why can't we also look at all the good things that happen to us and see them as a reward?

We're not all alike, here or on the Other Side, and it would be awful if we all were just globs of gooey goodness. We have our own personalities, and we're constantly shaped by life experiences and the opinions of others. But with a great deal of honesty—no holds barred—we can become the best that we can be at our own unique soul level.

Just think: If no one ever had a unique or conflicting point of view, we'd all be a bunch of robots cloned together . . . mindless and senseless. The greatest thinkers, speakers, and writers of all time were the ones who had the courage to step out and not only give their two cents' worth, but also support their position with logic and truth that we could understand.

The bottom line is: People will like you and love you if you're *real.* You can be irritating, aggravating, funny, and caustic, as long as it's really you. But I have to add that you must always be in a state of loving, and not in a state of *hoping,* to be loved. If you're in the state of loving, love will come to you.

Exercise

Each step in this eight-week course will include an exercise or two to get you thinking about who you really are. By completing these exercises thoughtfully and honestly, you'll learn how to be more *proactive* instead of being *reactive*—that is, you'll respond to events in your life in a positive way. So let's get started.

This first exercise will help you realize who you are. Now that you've had a chance to reflect on all the things you've been determined by, all the things that have been put on you, and all the things other people have told you, you're ready to explore your true essence. So take out a piece of paper (or better yet, turn to the first page of a blank journal) and divide it in half. On the top left-hand side, write "All the Things I'm Not." On the right-hand side, write "All the Things I Am." Here's an example for you to use as a guide:

All the Things I'm Not	All the Things I Am
I'm not passive.	I'm generous.
I'm not mean or vindictive.	I'm loving toward animals and most people.
I'm not insincere.	I'm creative.

In my case, I was trained to be a good little girl—to be quiet, sit in the corner, and not say anything unless I was spoken to. Is that really me? Of course not! After this list is complete, you may be pleasantly surprised, not only by your honesty, but by what the true essence of you—or your soul—is.

This will not only boost your estimation of yourself, but also release who you are deep inside.

Now again, divide a piece of paper in half, and this time, write on the left side the paper "Things I'd Like to Change about Myself." On the right side, write "Things I Want to Affirm in My Life." See the following example:

Things I'd Like to Change about Myself	Things I Want to Affirm in My Life
I'm too much of a perfectionist.	I'm upbeat.
I'm impatient with myself.	Children love me.
I procrastinate.	I have unique talents.

After you complete this list, see the areas that you need to work on, but also see the ways in which you're truly a good person. You might even notice that some of the traits you consider negative can be turned into a positive part of yourself.

After you've completed these exercises, repeat the following affirmation every day (or as often as needed) and practice the meditation to continue to bring your self-esteem to a higher level.

Affirmation

Each day, face yourself in the mirror and say: *"I am a happy, loving person, and I carry God's unique essence in my soul. Every action I do today will be for others as well as myself."*

Meditation

Lie in a prone position or sit comfortably in a chair. Begin to relax yourself from your toes up to your feet, legs, trunk, neck, arms, and head, and surround yourself with an emerald-green light for healing. Breathe deeply, and each time you exhale, say, "I am letting go of all negativity."

Now take yourself to a meadow. Walk slowly and feel your guides, your angels, and your loved ones who have passed over by your side. Notice that you feel free and light, almost as if you are glowing with

God's love, and you sense deep inside the true, happy, successful beauty of your immortal soul. You will begin to feel that all the guilt, determinism, opinions, criticisms, cruelty, and rejection you have stored up—all the negativity—is peeling off like so many heavy overcoats. You can even pick out specific embarrassing incidents, obsessions, losses, and pains, or you can just let them come. As soon as they do, mentally let them drop away.

You are still walking, and all of a sudden you come upon a stream. You step into it, and it feels cool on your feet. You follow this stream until you come upon a waterfall. Stepping under it, you notice that the water is cool, but not cold and as this water flows over your body, you feel the last remnants of any negativity gently rinse off.

The light coming through the waterfall makes a rainbow of color; and the blues, reds, yellows, and greens seem to flow through your body. The yellow and gold increase your spirituality, the blue calms your soul and relieves depression, and the red accelerates healing and blood flow to all parts of the body. The green light heals every part of your body, soul, and mind.

Stay under the waterfall as long as you wish, and then bring yourself back through the stream, across the meadow, and all the way back to yourself, feeling the very unique essence of you—the you that came to learn as well as give glory to God. Now come up, all the way up, feeling better than you've ever felt.

STEP 2

HOW TO BREAK THE PATTERNS THAT KEEP YOUR SOUL UNDER A BLANKET OF NEGATIVITY

We've all formed patterns and rituals throughout our entire life, whether it's cuddling a favorite teddy bear as we fall asleep at night or twirling our hair when we're nervous. There are certain things we habitually do when we get up in the morning, such as brushing our teeth and reading the paper, and other things we do before we go to bed, like making sure all the doors are locked or keeping a glass of water on the nightstand (as I do). These types of behaviors are usually automatic and comforting, and they make us feel stable. In fact, if one of these things gets out of sync, we may feel "off center" for the entire day.

You see, we all have a spiritual center for our soul, and the patterns we form are often positive coping mechanisms that keep us in balance when something makes us uncomfortable or afraid. Some of you may remember a comedian by the name of Don Knotts, who played Barney Fife on *The Andy Griffith Show*. When he started out, he had such horrible stage fright that it was paralyzing, so for his stand-up act on *The Steve Allen Show,* he portrayed a man giving a speech who was so nervous that he could barely talk, much less swallow. He twitched and jiggled, and everyone laughed because they could all identify with that phobia. Not until many years later did the public find out that this wasn't just Don's shtick, it was a real pattern that had plagued him most of his life—that is, until he decided to turn it into something positive. As he continued acting out his fear in front of an audience, his stage fright disappeared.

Negative Patterns and Bad Habits

Unfortunately, it sometimes happens that the coping skills we develop to deal with challenging situations are more destructive than the feelings of insecurity we're trying to avoid in the first place, and then, because we live in this house or temple that we call a *body,* these physical patterns affect our spiritual growth. We may delude ourselves into thinking that certain behaviors are positive mechanisms, because sometimes there's a fine line between a healthy habit and an obsessive one. For instance, it's hygienically mandatory to wash our hands before meals and after taking a trip to the restroom, but what if, like a client I had, we feel compelled to wash our hands 104 times a day? Any action, deed, or emotion—even a positive one— becomes destructive when pushed too far.

Observe yourself and others as you reinforce your chosen habits with your words and actions: "I can't live without my morning coffee," "I have to have a few cocktails to relax after a stressful day," "I always eat when I'm nervous [or happy or sad or whatever]," or "With my schedule, I need drugs to keep me at peak performance." Statements like these not only program your behavior, but justify it as well.

It takes some time and definitely some back-tracking to find the root or core of these negative patterns, or to determine when we first let them come into our consciousness. Many people in our society have developed the pattern of eating to comfort themselves, even though they know it's destructive, because they feel helpless and trapped in their body. Others form a pattern of drinking because they want to be accepted—maybe it makes them feel more socially "in." (And I'm not talking about a glass of wine at dinner—I'm referring to the folks who think they need a drink for courage or to get a buzz, and they don't stop.) And then there are those who decide to smoke because they want to be "cool," and just like alcohol, the cigarettes become a necessary companion. I'll say here, without reservation, that with "friends" like these, you don't need enemies!

Drugs, while more deadly (and make no mistake, they *are* deadly), have the same allure, and the same seduction: "I'll be part of the group," or "I'll escape my worries." Even prescription medications can be as lethal as any drug on the street when they're abused, but people often convince themselves that if their pills came from a pharmacy, they must be all right. This is a fool's paradise, because all these patterns are far more harmful than any insecurity we may have.

A less obvious habit that many people develop is that of being disappointed in themselves and beating themselves up. This is a behavior that may have started all the way back in childhood, or as recently as yesterday—anytime your expectations of yourself were greater than what you could accomplish: "I didn't pass the test, so I must be stupid," "I didn't win the game, which means I disappointed everyone," "I don't dress as well as everyone else, so I'm a nerd," "My brother can do everything better, which is why Mom and Dad like him better," "No matter what I try to do it fails, so I might as well give up," and strangely enough in this day of heightened awareness, "Nothing goes right for me, so I must be cursed."

We could go on and on with these mental patterns that take root, flavor our lives, and, if we let them, haunt us forever. Many times we make poor decisions in life because we settle for less, thinking we're unworthy. But we must remember that these behaviors aren't defects of our innate soul or self, they're simply part of life in the physical world.

The Hidden Meaning

Oscar Wilde once wrote a novel about a man named Dorian Gray. Briefly, it tells the story of a vain and evil man who has a portrait painted of himself. Each day that he lives, and with each perverse thing he does, the picture of him ages and becomes more and more grotesque, while Dorian himself remains young and handsome. As the portrait grows uglier, he hides it in a closet, because he knows it's a reflection of his true soul. Finally, Dorian tries to destroy the portrait, and ultimately turns horribly old and ugly and dies, while the picture returns to its beautiful, original form.

I've often thought about how this applies to all of us—not because we're evil, but because it's human nature to hide our negative behaviors or feelings in the closet and show the world another face. Sometimes we're afraid that someone will open up that secret door and expose the deep-seated fear or inadequacy that we don't want anyone to see. The fact is, many of our patterns can be sublimations for things that have deeper meanings. For instance, in my first marriage, I was an obsessive cleaning freak. (My father used to remark half-jokingly that I should just tie a mop to my rear end so I could walk and clean at the same time.) I now realize that my unhappiness was making me too eager to please—I was trying to perfect an outward environment because I couldn't seem to fix the negativity within my marriage.

On the one hand, sublimation is a great way to reduce fear and stress, but then you have to ask yourself why you don't just get rid of the *source* of the stress. I think the answer to this question is fairly straightforward: *Because it isn't always easy.* I had a college professor once ask, "Did you ever notice that the vision we have of ourselves when we're in our teens, especially when it's negative, is a hard pattern to break?" Over the years, I've thought a lot about that seemingly simple sentence, and I've realized how true it is. If we felt awkward or our complexion was bad or we struggled socially, we started forming patterns that became deeply rooted.

Here's a perfect example: I recently met with a client who was completely obsessed with her looks. She had every cream on the market, and had been through every surgery and laser treatment around. She was always looking in the mirror, and she picked herself apart relentlessly. It truly got to the point that her entire life was consumed with improving her physical appearance. This focus didn't have its roots in vanity, but in a sadness deep within her soul. She felt deficient and powerless inside, so she tried to make the outside better, hoping that this would help her improve how she felt.

The obsession with material wealth is another common behavioral trap. Some people decide somewhere along the line that money can solve their problems: "If I'm rich, no one can touch me," "I can buy happiness," or "People will look up to me if I have a lot of cash." Yet when you breathe your last breath and go to the Other Side, no one cares how many cars you had or how many facials you got—least of all you. Do I believe that God meant for each of us to look our best and be comfortable? You bet. But when your desire for wealth becomes all-consuming, then it's a sign that something deep inside is truly haywire, and your soul can't celebrate its unique life or find happiness in performing and learning for God.

Again, some of these behavior patterns operate on a subconscious level, while others are on a conscious level, but they all start with the soul's struggle to survive the game of life. In looking back at my own experience, I'm sure that I ended up where I am because I'm a humanitarian who wanted and still wants to "save" everyone, and that I formed my business due to this pattern of needing to help. In retrospect, I can see that I did it out of a desire for security. After all, not too many years ago (and to this day, in many places), being a psychic was an oddity, so I formed my foundation to support others like me. This made me feel more secure, and it also made me feel less strange, because all of a sudden I was surrounded by people who believed in me and my philosophy. Two things were accomplished: I encouraged other people, and I created my own niche, so it was a win-win situation. (My friends and business associates will attest to the fact that I've always said if everyone doesn't win, it's empty and useless.)

Breaking Bad Habits

Now it's time to clean house. I'm always amazed by how much time we spend on useless worries and thoughts. Yes, of course we pick our charts and all the good and bad that goes with them, but that's because we're here to learn. So again, when we discover the imprints of negative patterns in our lives, we should make a concerted effort to monitor what we don't like and keep what's good.

How many of *your* patterns—especially the exhausting ones or those that are harmful to your mind, soul, and body—would you like to break? Has telling lies been a pattern in your life? Do you do it for fear of being disliked or getting yelled at? Do you do it to make yourself feel more important? Whatever the underlying meaning, it will come forward if you ask yourself honestly why you feel the need to be deceitful.

Do you have a pattern of putting other people down? Does doing so make you feel superior or more in control? Spreading gossip falls under the same category. It's a habit people get into when they want to make others think they have the inside track, or that they're some kind of oracle of hidden knowledge that should be shared—even at the expense of others' feelings. The old adage holds true—if you don't have something good (or even validly true in a positive way) to say, it's better not to say anything at all. Does this mean you can't vent about hurts, wrongful actions, or unjust conditions in the world? Of course not, and I believe that there are people who are just evil and should be exposed for wrongful acts—that's what justice is about.

Be an investigative thinker. Think back to the first time you felt inadequate, stupid, insincere, or rejected, and ask yourself, "What event introduced this emotion into my life?" Try to remember what verbiage was used that made you feel in any way "less" than before. Do your best to determine why this message stuck with you, and why you accepted it as a negative pattern, while others slid off.

Then, the next time you catch yourself repeating a negative pattern, try this short exercise: Tell your mind, "Stop!" Instead of continuing with your usual behavior, take yourself mentally to a mountaintop and lean against a pine tree. Look at the beautiful view that spreads out in front of you, feel the sun on your face, and listen to the birds. If you do this enough times, you'll break the synaptic impulses that keep playing the same record over and over in your mind.

Here's another short exercise that really helps: After you've asked yourself when this pattern (whether it's physical or mental) started, and you get a real handle on where it comes from, you can begin to release any negative emotion you had attached to it. Think of the habit as a recorded cassette tape, and press your forefinger to your forehead and say "Eject!" This serves two purposes: (1) You acknowledge your negative behaviors; and (2) you make a new imprint on your subconscious—that is, you're creating a new pattern to eradicate the problem.

In other words, take a pattern you recognize that's harmful to your mental and physical well-being and substitute a productive one in its place. (That's what Nicorette gum does. It not only releases nicotine, but it gives a person something to do with his or her mouth besides smoke.)

In place of your old behavior, develop a new hobby. When I get overwhelmed, I do crafts. One particularly stressful year, I made 12 needlepoint

Santa stockings! It gave me a great deal of pleasure to hand them out at Christmastime, and it really relieved my stress. If you feel particularly obsessive, take a walk. Any diversion will eventually break a negative pattern if done often enough, for it allows you to relax enough to let in a productive one.

When we've done something good and noble, we should also use that opportunity to form a pattern of being proud of ourselves. This isn't ego or vanity, even though we sometimes feel awkward when we're complimented or have accomplished a particular feat. Let's not negate the positive things we do; instead, let's keep striving for excellence and approval in a right and just way.

We're all born with talents and imperfections that we have to learn from, but the shortcomings can be transformed into power once we face our so-called dragons. My grandmother used to say, "Within your weakness lies your strength, sleeping." We have to address the fact that we have negative patterns, and we always have the ability to develop positive new ones. This makes our soul happy, quiet, and in harmony with our chart.

Exercise

Divide a piece of paper into two columns. On the left side, write down the negative habits you wish to rid yourself of. On the right side of the paper, put in a positive substitution (this can be something physical or mental). See the example below:

Negative Pattern to Get Rid of	Positive Substitution
Obsessing over my ex	Every time I start to have obsessive thoughts about my ex, I'll get on the tread-mill for ten minutes.
Excessive snacking	Whenever I feel the urge to snack, I'll drink a glass of water and then go outside for some fresh air instead.
Yelling at my kids	If I get to the point where I'm about to scream at my children, I'll go into the bathroom and be silent for one minute.

This list can help you find the harmful patterns that you perpetuate. Sometimes it's difficult to come up with an appropriate substitute, but be honest and work hard at it anyway. The affirmation that follows will reinforce this change.

Affirmation

Every day, say to yourself: *"Not only is today a new day, but it is the day that my inner soul strength comes to my consciousness, helping me conquer all my negative patterns. With God's help, all is possible!"*

Meditation

First, ask yourself when this pattern of low self-esteem, obsessive worry, or habitual behavior took hold of you. Then put yourself in a quiet state of relaxation and breathe in deeply. Take eight deep breaths, and with each breath say, "I am reaffirming my soul's goal to learn my lessons, without any negative behavioral overlays that I may have absorbed through word or deed. I will not only erase and release any adversity, but I will replace it with positive patterns so my soul can grow and flourish."

Stay relaxed and let any scenario come up to your consciousness. Ask that you be shown, through visualization or a sense of feeling, where these negative patterns began to take root, and put them in the white, purifying light of the Holy Spirit. Also ask that for each destructive habit, your guide and angels show you how to replace these hurtful imprints with healing actions and affirmations.

Now see yourself in a beautiful meadow. It is filled with flowers, and trees border the edge of this spacious land. You lie down in the flowers, and the sweet, heady smell of roses, gardenias, or whatever fragrance you love fills your senses. In the sky above, you begin to see different shapes in the clouds, which seem to depict different episodes from your life and what has affected you. Once you have had a chance to observe each scene, you will release it and watch as the wind breaks up the clouds. Every time you do this, your soul feels lighter.

Lie there as long as you wish, breathing in the nature around you and letting go of everything that bothers you. Then bring yourself out of the meadow and feel free.

STEP 3

HOW TO UNLOCK THE MEMORIES OF PAST LIVES AND UTILIZE THEM TO MAKE YOU SPIRITUALLY WELL

Unlike the patterns discussed in Step 2 (those that originated sometime between childhood and adulthood), there are many

phobias, everyday fears, and incessant worries that don't relate to this lifetime. Many times I've worked with people who were baffled by anxieties that seemed to have no basis—in other words, they couldn't be tracked through therapy or by their own investigation into their past. In these types of situations, we've had to go back even further and do what I call a "deep search" into a person's overall chart, because the cause of the uneasiness resides somewhere in the cells of his or her mind and body.

Uncovering Past-Life Traumas

I once had a client who drove under the same overpass every day for 20 years on her way to work. One day as she was approaching it, she broke out in a sweat and felt as if she couldn't breathe—she was sure she was having a heart attack. She turned around and headed for the emergency room, where she was told she was "just having an anxiety attack." (Those words, "*just . . . an anxiety attack,*" *just* make me crazy. If you've ever had one—and very few people *haven't* had a form of this at one time or another—then you know that it can be the most frightening and debilitating experience you'll ever go through. Usually it comes out of the blue, unbidden and without warning. You can't "cause" one, it just happens. But back to my client . . .)

When this woman came to see me, I directed her via meditation to return to another time. When she did, she remembered being trapped under an old bridge in Pennsylvania back in the early 1800s. She was buried under heavy beams and rubble, and she died there. The amazing thing was that in her previous life, she passed away at the same age she'd now reached in this life—which explained why the phobia hit when it did. After we did the guided meditation, she lost her fear and could go under the overpass again.

Another time, I got a visit from the frantic mother of a three-year-old. She came to see me because every time she turned on the shower, her little daughter would scream, "No, Mama! Don't!" The mother resorted to taking baths, but still needed help because whenever anyone else in the family took a shower, or her daughter even *heard* a shower, the young child would panic. Through my psychic sense, I immediately knew what the problem was, without even questioning the little girl: She'd been in Nazi Germany, and had been one of the women who was killed after being herded into what seemed like a shower, but was really a gas chamber. I instructed the mom to go into the girl's room after the child went to sleep and tell her that the time of being afraid of showers was over, and that whatever she remembered happened in a past time, and that she was safe now. Within a week, the daughter was free of her fear of showers.

Life is like a record with different grooves, and sometimes the needle slips. What we have to do to keep the soul safe from a negative fear that's no longer relevant is *release* it. This is called "pulling the plug" on a negative past-life implant. When my own children had night terrors, I did the same thing I instructed the woman with the three-year-old to do: I just went in and told them that they were in this time, and what they were afraid of was in the past, long ago. When you do this, it isn't necessary to go through gruesome details. The soul mind knows exactly what you're talking about, and it will surrender the offending fear that blocks it from being free.

This was the case with a four-year-old boy I worked with who was just fine until the day his dad bought a telescope and set it up in the living room of the house. The little boy wandered into the room, saw the telescope, fell to the floor, and had some kind of seizure. Of course his mother and father took him to countless doctors, none of whom could find anything physically wrong with the child. Finally, they visited one of the M.D.'s I happen to work with, and he told the mother to take her son to see me. She apprehensively made an appointment, and as soon as I saw her son, I psychically realized that he'd experienced a recent death. He'd been in a submarine, and when a torpedo hit, he'd been pinned beneath a periscope (which looked a lot like a telescope to the little boy).

I put the child in a relaxed state and told him not to be afraid. I reassured him that whatever he was afraid of had happened *before,* and that now he was in *this* time, where nothing would harm him. This was the end of the seizures for the little boy—he's never had another.

Releasing the Past, Healing the Present

You can and should explore your memories—both from this life and any past lives—and be investigative enough to see what you learn from them. But analyzing isn't enough—you also have to neutralize any challenge by asking for release. By doing so, you may even discover how you can turn negative events into opportunities for positive growth. (Let me also say here that I'm the first one to recommend that you seek therapy if needed.)

Let's say that you're dealing with physical or mental abuse. In fact, I'll use my own life as an example. It's no secret that my mother was a master at insidious emotional battery. I had a choice: I could have adopted her behavior, but instead I went 180 degrees so I'd be different from her. I often thank her—and I even did so when she was alive—because without this negative example, I might have not been the caring mother I am today. I never told my mother *why* I was thankful for her, because it was enough that God and I knew.

The hurts we carry in life can't be covered up with Band-Aids. Like physical wounds, these sore spots can only heal when the air hits them. Yet while it's important to acknowledge and let out the pain so that it doesn't fester, it's equally imperative that we adjust our behavior to release the past and move on.

I had a friend who talked incessantly about abandonment issues. In almost every experience she had, she felt left behind. The irony is that by obsessively discussing this matter, she seemed to draw more of it to her, and after hearing her go on about it so much, I also wanted to run away! Her story really reinforces the age-old truth that thoughts and words become realities. We can all definitely set ourselves up to fulfill our own prophecies.

I see this all the time with my clients. The very thing that haunts them from this life (as well as in their past lives) is what they continue to run right into time and again. Don't feel bad if this happens to you, because we get stuck in this rut from time to time, but to keep embracing it does stop the soul from growing. For example, a male friend of mine whose wife had left him was determined to hang on to the relationship—even though she went back and forth from her lover to him. His excuse for not getting on with his life was, in his own words, "The fear of rejection." What he didn't realize was that he was already living a life of total rejection, and he was the one keeping himself in that place.

I recently heard a comforting story about a woman who had a very real near-death experience. She went through a beautiful bright light and felt completely elated, and then she was met by a gorgeous, radiant being. She exclaimed, "I don't know if I'm good enough to be here!" The being responded, "We expect you to spill the milk, but it's really how you clean it up that matters." How simple, yet how true. That statement really brings home the words of Jesus, that if we become more like little children, the kingdom of heaven will be ours.

Don't get me wrong—there isn't anything easy about mulling over the painful parts of your life, but you have to ask yourself: "Do I want to be enslaved by my memories, or do I want to simply see them as episodes that, painful as they are, have helped me gain strength and become who I am today?" If you do the latter, you'll be able to gaze into the mirror and know that you've survived the good and the bad, and you'll be freer and even stronger for it.

Creating Joyful Memories

We've spent a lot of time discussing negative memories, so how about taking some time to address all the *good* memories we have. For me, those are the times I've shared with my psychic grandmother, my friends, my children, my teachers, and my clients. Even holding my grandchildren's hands—these are life's precious moments. When we make love happen, we allow our soul to grow beyond all the weeds of bad memories.

Unlike replacing harmful habits with healthy patterns, you can't just swap a hurtful memory with a pleasant one. But when you take a balanced look at the positive and the negative in your life, then you can take pride in not only what you've overcome, but what you've *become* because of the sum of all your experiences. Learn, for example, to say, "I've been abused, *but* there was a time when life was happy. I can and will recapture that feeling without remorse or pain. I refuse to substitute a false sense of security for happiness, and I won't be afraid to be alone, because I know that I'm always surrounded by God, my guide, the angels, and all my loved ones who have passed over to the Other Side. I will replace any negativity that's attached to bad memories, and repeat to myself: *It was only a learning process. I have been loved, and I can love.*"

Exercise

Divide a sheet of paper in two. Put all your "Painful Memories" on the left side of the page and all your "Positive Memories" on the right. This time, at the bottom of the page on the left side, draw conclusions—in other words, what did you learn from these experiences? Don't worry if an answer doesn't come right away; it will if you're persistent. It doesn't matter how many pages you use, just ask your soul and God to give you insight into why you suffered. You'll get the answers. Here's an example:

Painful Memories	Positive Memories
When my third-grade teacher called me stupid	When I got an A on a term paper
The time I felt everyone was talking about me at the office	Last week when a stranger smiled at me at the grocery store
My parents' divorce	My last family vacation

I learned that adults don't always have the right answers, and that I need to base my self-worth on what *I* think of me, not what others say.

Affirmation

Each day, say to yourself: *"When life gives me pits, I'll plant them and grow cherry trees."*

Meditation

Lie or sit in a comfortable position and surround yourself with golden light. Again, start relaxing your body, beginning with your feet and going all the way up your legs, trunk, shoulders, arms, neck, and head. Keep breathing in and out. Now say: "I am unstressing every part of my body. I can address every cell and tell each of them to work in harmony." You are the guardian of your own mind, body, and soul, and you can instruct your mind to release any and all negativity attached to a horrifying or unpleasant memory—whether it's from this life or any past time. Let yourself relax even more deeply so that you feel as if you are floating.

All of a sudden, you are aware that you are floating through a beautiful white tunnel. You feel no pain, only a sense of peace and well-being. All your worries and hurtful memories evaporate now, like smoke. As you progress through this tunnel, you feel an even stronger connection to your real soul than ever before, and you realize that you are the sum total of all your experiences. The layers of self-doubt, envy, inadequacy, worry, depression, and vengeance all become nothing more than a part of a play you saw but left behind.

As you reach the end of the tunnel, you are bathed in the purple light of spirituality. Now you find yourself facing a beautiful Romanesque building with marble pillars and stairs going up. You ascend these steps and go through the marble archway. Everything is gleaming and white, and in the middle of a room at the top of the stairs, there is a beautiful orblike glass. You approach it and look into it. At first it seems opaque, but then images begin to take shape, and you realize that you are scanning your life. You see how you chose your chart and what lessons you wanted to learn. Then more images come very quickly, but sequentially . . . your birth, your early childhood, your puberty. Stop at any place you wish to linger. See the painful as well as the joyful.

When you reach a sad or very upsetting period, realize that it was a learning process. You can even refer to your chart, and you'll be surprised by how much you decided to learn. Notice that as you watch, you feel disconnected. It is you, but you are past that now. Even if you cry at the sad times, this is a release.

You can even look into this glass orb to view past lives and let go of any phobias or illnesses that you might have brought over. Stay as long as you want—believe me, it will go faster than you imagine. Hold on to the pleasant memories you view, for they make you smile. When you have had enough of the scanning, you can always go back through the archway, the steps, and even the tunnel, but with the realization that you

*have pulled out the negative memories that
were stalling your soul, and brought forth
joyful recollections into your reality.*

*Bring yourself back, all the way back,
feeling free, released, and in full control of
your true self. You are on track and very
much loved by God.*

STEP 4

HOW TO INCITE YOUR SOUL TO SPIRITUALITY AND BECOME EVEN MORE PSYCHIC

So far, we've covered some of the aspects of removing negative patterns, memories, and behavioral overlays, whereby our souls can become unfettered and expand so that they magnify God's love. Now let's get down to the often-misunderstood concept called *spirituality*. What it *isn't* is "religionistic," yet that doesn't mean we can't be Christian, Buddhist, Jewish, or any other faith. It just means that our spirits, in their total individuality, are seeking their own truths, and many times this goes beyond simply following the dogma of a particular church.

If we get too wrapped up in human-made doctrine, we become mired in rules and regulations. These decrees have nothing to do with what Christ, Siddhārtha (Buddha), Muhammed, or any of the other entities sent by God came to teach us. Their purpose was to relieve humankind of so many of the overlays that we've addressed in the previous steps in this book.

You see, we can be any sect or any number of righteous denominations and still be spiritual. Individual beliefs are only different pathways, all leading to God. Our Creator doesn't stand in judgment and say that we can only come to Him if we're Protestant; we can be Mormon, Baha'i, or any faith we choose. It also doesn't matter what we call God, whether it's Yahweh, Jehovah, or Allah. God is the Supreme Creator, the *Primium Mobile* (which means "Unmoved Mover").

If we do a little research into the history of how the world's religions started, we'll notice that nearly all of them began with a messenger, an avatar, or a prophet. Then, when we go to the original spiritual texts, we'll find another common thread, which is a simple message that governs basic human laws, ethics, and righteousness: Love God, do as much good as you can for others and yourself, and then go home.

Getting Outside of Yourself

One of the most important spiritual tenets is to *know yourself*. It seems fairly straightforward, doesn't it? Well, actually, it's probably one of the most difficult, complex things we may ever attempt. In my years of working with hundreds of thousands of people, I've become convinced that the only way we can really do this is to interact with others. I know this may fly in the face of much of what we've been told or taught, and I don't mean that we shouldn't care for or love ourselves, but too much self-searching leads to self-indulgence (besides being boring and providing no means to any end). If we live our life by giving to and serving those around us, we become less phobic, less ill, and less isolated, and we begin to have broader, less self-centered goals. This is what really makes us more spiritual.

We're meant to be social entities interacting with and reacting to others in a positive way, and we're designed to be outward and giving—otherwise we wouldn't have arms and hands that hold, ears and eyes that hear and see our world, and a mouth that can speak words of kindness and offer assistance. If we don't value our relationships with other people, then we might as well have been created as a tube with rollers. I'm not saying that I don't love time alone, but it should be spent in a productive manner—getting involved in a hobby, writing, listening to tapes or music, or even day-dreaming.

If we're too focused on how everything affects us, we can become anxious and neurotic. Indeed, the word *occult,* which means "secretive, hidden, and reclusive," doesn't just describe religious groups or sects, but it can apply to us individually as well. If we're left to our own thoughts, with no ambitions or concerns except those that directly affect us, we'll find that eventually we'll be nothing but miserable. But if we have a higher goal of loving God and approaching this life as an in-service workshop to learn for the glory of our soul, we can be alone for a while, yet we'll always have the knowledge that the whole purpose of coming here was to give a blessing to another person's life. If we accept this "magnificent obsession"—that is, helping others and growing spiritually—we'll truly grow to know ourselves.

In addition, dealing with other people trains us to improve ourselves in every situation. Sometimes, those around us will make us impatient, so we'll have the opportunity to learn patience. We may see prejudice, so we'll become understanding and know that we're all equal. Our experiences will teach us honesty, because if we're not truthful, our deceit always comes back to us. We'll learn justice, righteousness, and even tolerance. If we're not subjected to anything or anyone but ourselves, what reflection do we have to grow from? How will we learn to live with honesty and without hypocrisy unless we go through life and get burned now and then, which teaches us to avoid the hellfire of negativity that exists only on this plane?

When we deal with people in a helpful, caring capacity, it's almost as if a blessing falls over us like a mantle, and when we take care of God's creatures and creations, God will take care of us. Does that mean that our lives will always be full of nothing but joy and happiness? Of course not, but we'll be able to cope with disappointments and sadness. Think of John Walsh, the creator of TV's *America's Most Wanted,* who turned the pain of losing his son into positive energy by tracking down other fugitives who prey on people. Likewise, Mothers Against Drunk Driving (MADD) was started by two women, Cindi Lamb (whose infant daughter was permanently disabled in an accident caused by a driver under the influence of alcohol) and Candace Lightner (whose teenage daughter was killed by a drunk driver with multiple previous convictions), who turned their heartache into something productive that continues to yield great good.

Finally, getting outside of ourselves means letting go of impotent worry. Worry without action is nothing but damaging. Do we want to waste our time agonizing over scenarios that may never occur? That's an exercise in futility. Taking action when we're faced with actual challenges that can be tackled, on the other hand, is productive. So, for instance, rather than carrying on about your health, get yourself checked out by a doctor. Instead of getting yourself worked up about whether a friend is mad at you, ask if anything is wrong. And don't get distressed when your spouse isn't his or her usual self. Instead, investigate the cause of the change. Some people avoid this direct approach, claiming, "What I don't know can't hurt me." Well, if that's so, then how come they said this in the first place? Could it be that they're secretly stewing about something rather than facing it head-on?

Tapping In to Your Psychic Gifts

As we thread through the tapestry of life, we weave into it many colors and textures, and it's up to us to either make it beautiful or let it get frayed and threadbare. As we get to know ourselves and our reactions to various situations, we can begin to throw away what we don't want and keep what we find good in ourselves, because we'll know what gives us righteous anger, what makes us happy or sad, and so on. When you know *you*, all your psychic channels open up.

The dictionary's definition of *psychic* is "the power of discernment." Usually it's the power to see, sense, or feel without any tangible clue. It's a skill that may come on quickly—sometimes without rhyme or reason. Whether you call it intuition, a hunch, or a sense of "remembering," it's a gift that comes from God. As you become more helpful and outgoing, your spirituality will increase and your ability to sense and know will just come naturally. If you're shy or introverted, then start by connecting with just one kind individual you feel comfortable with—perhaps a child or an older person. Then you can start asking yourself questions. We've often been told not to trust our first impressions, but this is so wrong. Take whatever comes to you, and if you can't say it out loud, record it in a journal.

Don't be discouraged if at first you get some inaccurate information—or no response at all. Even nothing can be an answer—maybe nothing's going on! Again, take your first impression. Use the following categories for questions, and be open to any other messages that come in as well:

- Career
- Family
- Finances
- Health
- Loved Ones Who Have Passed Over

- Negative People
- Relationships
- Social Life
- Spirituality

If you feel a sense of brightness, as if your psychic sense has been activated, then go further and ask, "Who does this message pertain to?" Jot down your answers: Is the person short, medium, or tall; are they from the past, present or future? In general, time can be hard to determine, so when you're trying to figure out anything that has to do with a specific chronology, ask yourself if it feels immediate or further away. Start by counting months, seasons, years, and you'll find that one answer will feel better, or more "on."

This is a simple way to start, but it begins to exercise the muscle that I believe lies in what we call the "limbic brain," which is a part of our mind that most scientists don't understand. I'm convinced that this is the location of our third eye, on the right side of our head above the ear—also known as the "dead zone."

Of course, this part of our mind isn't really dead, it just lies dormant until we open the door. Actually, we use it all the time and don't even realize it. For instance, have you ever said to a friend, "What's on your mind? You're not yourself today." You may notice that something is different only moments after you see her. Perhaps she seems happy and full of life and then she admits that she's in love. Or he may seem down or depressed, and then tell you that he has a horrendous migraine or problems at home.

Naysayers will claim that you're just picking up on body language, but if that's the case, then how can my son and I and so many other psychics do readings over the phone—especially when the caller hasn't said anything more than "Hello"? The fact is that anyone can open their psychic channels anywhere and at any time—all they have to do is simply ask themselves a question and take their first answer or impression.

There are two main factors that prevent people from using their psychic sense more often. One is the fear of being wrong. Yet what someone says no to now may turn out to be true later. The person being read doesn't know the future yet, so if you get a "hit," stick with it. Can you be mistaken? Of course you can—only God is always right. But if you follow your instincts, you'll be accurate more often than not, and the more you practice, the better you'll get.

The other thing that makes people shy away from their innate psychic abilities is that many times the first impressions they get seem negative. That's because this is a negative planet, so things of that nature travel faster on this plane. When you get a discordant feeling or sensation, see if you can help the person concerned—don't just let your intuition lie dormant because of your fear.

You should also avoid reading for people who are close to you. If you do, you'll be unsuccessful because you'll become too emotionally involved and won't be able to be objective. The main thing is to remove yourself from sentimental situations. Once your ego gets in there, or your own problems, you're no longer functional or valid.

Everyone who deals with people on a spiritual or ethical basis should move above their own "stuff" and look at each person neutrally. I knew a psychic once who said that everyone had cancer. Guess who had it? That's right, *he* did. Another reader I knew was going through a divorce, and subsequently, she was sure that everyone she saw was going to be involved in a painful breakup. In truth, she was projecting her own issues onto everyone else. And on and on the story goes.

Here's a final caution: Whenever you take, you must also give back in comparable measure. So if you're doing readings for financial gain only, or to satisfy your own ego, then you're doomed to failure. It's spiritual law.

Exercise

Again, divide a paper into two columns, and call one "Acts I'm Not Proud Of" and the other "Acts I'm Proud Of." In your mind, go through the events of today only, and fill in each column with the actions you performed that either made you feel uplifted or disappointed you. See the following example.

Acts I'm Not Proud Of	Acts I'm Proud Of
I snapped at a store clerk for no good reason.	I told my co-worker that I appreciate her.
I made a rude gesture at the driver in the car next to me.	I let someone go ahead of me in the grocery line.
I didn't allow myself time to read the new book I've been wanting to start.	I ate a healthy and delicious lunch.

If you've been keeping a journal of your progress, be sure that at the end of this week you take a few minutes to flip through it and notice how you're getting more tuned in to your spirituality, and in turn, more free to express yourself. You'll also find that throughout this week, the list of things you're proud of will get longer, while the left column will get shorter. That's because your passion to help yourself and others will really take root in your soul.

Affirmation

Each day, say to yourself: *"I am from the Divine source, a unique spark from the Divine sparkler."*

Meditation

Relax, and situate yourself in a comfortable chair or lie down. Surround yourself with not only white light, but rose-colored light as well. (White symbolizes purity and rids us of negativity, while rose-colored light is love.) Feel this light coming up through your feet and legs as you relax your entire body. Breathe deeply as all negativity flows out of you like dark smoke and the rose light of love takes its place. Still breathing regularly and gently, as you do when you are asleep, visualize the light moving up your body, all the way to your neck, arms, and face—even behind your eyes. The last vestiges of any and all negativity are being absorbed in the light of the Holy Spirit and God's light of love.

Now imagine that you are in a desert. The sand seems to stretch as far as you can see. The amazing part is that you are not hot, and you have no sense of isolation even though there is a starkness about your environment. Everything is serene, and as you sense the wind shift slightly and feel the sand beneath your feet, you begin to notice that this simplicity helps you unclutter your mind.

Imagine the peace, the quiet, the wind, the sand . . . and walking effortlessly. All of a sudden, over a sand dune to your right, you begin to see what looks like the top of a pyramid. You climb the dune, and there in the middle of the desert is a gleaming pyramid. It looks like a prism, and colors of every description emanate from it whenever the sunlight changes.

You rush over to it and notice that it has indented levels you can climb. You are not sure at first why you want to climb this ancient structure, but you feel a reverence, and you see the structure as a symbol of knowledge. You climb to the top, and when you reach the very apex, you ask God to infuse you with not only spirituality, but the power of discernment—the power of prophecy.

As soon as you ask, you feel that your mind and soul have opened. It is as if you have become a beautiful tube—not a mindless tube, but a conduit for God's knowledge and the line that taps in to life's records.

Make a prayerful mental contract: "I will never use the knowledge I receive for my own gain. I will never use it to hurt anyone through spite, vengeance, jealousy, or malice of any kind. I will ask that my tube stays pure, and that each day I grow in spiritual grace and be inspired to help people."

During this period, you may ask about any person or problem that you need clarity about. You may be surprised by how immediate the answer is. Remember, this is not for your own gain, but to make you better able to help others. If a challenge is clouding your mind, ask that it be resolved.

Take yourself down from the pyramid knowing that you can go there anytime you want. Eventually, you will be able to do it (that is, receive the infusion of knowledge) on command, but it never hurts to have a vehicle to get there. Bring yourself

across the sand and back to this world,
feeling absolutely refreshed and free.

STEP 5

HOW TO PREVENT MATERIAL GAIN FROM DOMINATING YOUR LIFE, AND INSTEAD, LIVE COMFORTABLY AND BE SPIRITUALLY RICH

Boy, that's a mouthful! Let's begin by taking it apart: Is there really anything wrong with wanting a comfortable, secure future?

No—it's only when material gain becomes an obsession or a passion unto itself that it muddles our mind and soul. Should we like nice things? Of course we should. I can't believe that God would have put all these beautiful creations in this world if we weren't intended to enjoy them. But when making money for money's sake is our only goal, then we begin to head off-track. In other words, if we have to spend cash to make us happy, to buy love or friendship, or to create some false image of ourselves, then we'd better adjust our motives and thinking processes.

Too Much of a Good Thing

Money has never been the root of all evil—in fact, even the Bible says it's the *love of money* that's the root of all kinds of evil. Only when it's hoarded and adored, creating greed and avarice, is it a bad thing. When used properly, it's a tool to make life easier, to pay your bills, and to help others.

Over the years, I've worked extensively with both the "haves" (those who are rich in terms of worldly goods) and the "have nots" (those who tend to struggle financially), and I've found that neither group is immune to material concerns. The folks that have money are often worried about keeping it, and the ones who don't have it are usually obsessed with getting it. I believe that you can always spot those who live paycheck to paycheck, not because this is necessarily such a terrible situation to be in, but because these people tend to hate their circumstances and it shows. You see, there's a spiritual light that emanates from us when we're dedicated to life and what it has to offer, and constant financial worries can dull this light.

Some anxiety about debt is bad enough, but when we become fixated on money to the exclusion of what's true, eternal, and lasting, then we're really in over our heads. There's a word for those who fail to value inner qualities and instead place all attention on outward wealth: *materialistic*. Webster's dictionary says that materialism is "a theory that physical matter is the only or fundamental reality and all being and processes and phenomena can be explained as manifestations or results of matter," and "a preoccupation with or stress upon material rather than intellectual or spiritual things." The problem with placing all our values on what we can acquire is that we'll never be satisfied, because we could always have *more*.

Sadly, not only have we become a society of "I want more," but now we want someone to give it to us. So many want to start at the top, without putting in the effort required to be successful—financially or otherwise. Some people say that this excessive materialism is the fault of the family, the media, or the community, and perhaps there's a degree of truth in all the above. But the main problem is that we've lost our spiritual zeal.

People have said to me, "I feel better when I'm buying things, even if I know I'll regret it later." For these folks, spending money provides a kind of rush or high—a feeling of excitement to cover up something inside that's lonely, frightened, or without any self-worth. Yet the reality of the matter is that no matter how hard we try, we can't improve our lives by adorning ourselves on the outside, whether it's where we live, the jewelry we wear, or the things we possess. We can try for a "quick fix" or a temporary face-lift, but the relief those measures provide only lasts for so long.

Money and what it buys can help us put up a facade to fool other people, but when we feel poor in spirit, there's no amount of cash that can fill that void. Ironically, we often hear people say that they were happier when they had less. Why is that? Maybe because they didn't get so wrapped up in "things" that they forgot about what really matters. There have even been surveys conducted among people who won the lottery, and believe it or not, a few years later, an overwhelming number of these "lucky" winners are bankrupt and alone. Does that mean we should all just give up and go live in a box? No, that's ridiculous. We all want to have enough to pay our bills, take care of our loved ones, and be comfortable. But aside from meeting those basic needs, what would we do with a ton of money?

Some people use their extra cash to "buy" their children. For example, they'll say, "I'm too busy to spend time with you, so here's a new video game. Now go entertain yourself." This gives our kids the message that we don't want to be bothered. Others do the same with their significant other: "Here's a Rolex—now you know I love you," or "Honey, this new car shows I care." It isn't wrong to give gifts to the people we love, but things shouldn't take the place of communication and intimacy.

We all need to ask ourselves why we spend any of our time worrying about how we'll keep up with the neighbors, how we're judged by our salary or who we work for, or whether we're from "old money" or "new money" (whatever that really means). As I stated before, most of us have more than we actually need, and we buy more than we can ever eat or wear.

Case in point: Six years ago, my son bought me a house. I truly love it, especially since my grandkids have practically been raised in it, but one day I was thinking, *How much of my house do I really occupy?* Most people make good use of a kitchen, bedroom, bathroom, and den if they have one. But beyond that, do we really need all this space?

(I practically live in my den: I write there, read there, watch TV there, go to the refrigerator there, and use the bathroom right next to it. Beats me what anyone else is doing in the rest of the house, and usually—except when the kids are there—I couldn't care less!) Certainly there's a point of comfort or even a measure of luxury . . . and then there's obscene extravagance.

The words "I just can't live without it" floor me. We should be looking to love and honor people—to foster friendship, fidelity, and loyalty—these are the rules of life. If others only love us for what we can give or buy them, then we should, like Jesus said, "Shake the dust off [and walk away]."

A Healthy Balance

My car is a purple VW Beetle. It gets great mileage, requires virtually no upkeep, takes me everywhere, and can fit into just about any parking space. While it's true that my choice in automobiles isn't just a matter of practicality (it's also a matter of taste), I don't see the point in spending a ton of money on a vehicle. I mean, come on, have you ever heard of anyone on their deathbed who wished they had driven a more expensive car?

It doesn't really matter what you drive or where you live, as long as you're full of joy and happiness and not trying to live beyond your means. (After all, who wants to spend their entire life playing catch-up with bill collectors and the IRS?) You can and should take care in your financial planning—building, buying, making yourself comfortable, and being just a little bit extravagant from time to time—so long as you realize that you're only leasing what you have in life. You don't own it, and you never will. It's all fleeting.

Clearly, if spending money and shopping are the only things that make you happy, then your soul is very poor. You can enrich yourself by reaching out to others—going to visit a home for the elderly, reading to children, or offering solace to a friend. Think back to the times that are precious to you, and notice how much the materialism around you mattered at those moments. When you gaze into a lover's eyes or hold a child in your arms, do you care if you're in an Armani suit or have a tiara on your head?

Perhaps you've had the experience of meeting someone whose mind, soul, and essence were so entrancing that you'd be hard-pressed to remember what they wore, what they drove, or even where they lived. Now don't get me wrong: We need hygiene; some pride in our personal appearance; and, in my case, an environment that's bug free! (As my grandmother used to say, "There's nothing wrong with being poor, but no one has to be dirty.") But as the saying goes, it's what's *inside* that really counts.

Consider the ancient Egyptians, whom I've studied for decades. They were so concerned about material possessions that they were buried with all their wealth. Still, they couldn't take it with them, and neither can we. When we make it a point to enjoy our lives, live within our means, and enjoy our loved ones and the spiritual riches that friendships and loyalty bring us, we feel very blessed and wealthy in our beliefs.

Getting What You Really Need

My grandfather Marcus Coil was a very wealthy man who lost it all in the big stock market crash of 1929. Instead of wasting his time despairing over his change in fortune, he turned to my grandmother and said, "Well, I learned how to make it once, so I'll just go out and make it again."

Even though the country was in the Great Depression and jobs were hard to come by, my grandfather put on a freshly pressed shirt and went to sit in the office of the gas company in Kansas City, Missouri, to look for work. He did this every day for a year, until finally, the head of the company came out and said, "Mr. Coil, anyone with your tenacity deserves a try." In six months my grandfather was the head of the company's entire Midwestern district.

The path to material gain begins with figuring out what it is you want to do with your life, or what gives you joy. I often hear people say, "I'd love to do such-and-such, but it doesn't pay enough." I remember a client of mine who loved animals but felt that just taking them in wouldn't afford her any money. "Why don't you start a small grooming business and then grow it into a kennel?" I suggested. Well, lo and behold, today she has a successful grooming business and not only boards animals, but breeds them as well.

If you have the vision and the goal, success will follow. Not everyone knows this, but I started out by taking out a loan on my car and hanging a shingle on a two-room office space with a couch, a couple of chairs, and a desk. At least six members of my old-time staff can attest to this. Even to this day, my ministers will affirm that we've seen times when meeting the payroll seemed impossible, but it has always come through. It's like the voice says in the movie *Field of Dreams:* "If you build it, they will come." Be the best at what you choose, go the extra mile, and life will reward you.

People have told me, "Sure, it was easy for you." How? I was just a Catholic-Jewish-Episcopalian girl from Kansas City whose father was a mailman and whose mother didn't work. How did that give rise to who I am today? The fact is, I decided to be a teacher, and I was. I wanted a foundation for spirituality, so I worked for it. I wanted to write, and I have and always will.

After you've set your goals, ask for what you *require,* not necessarily what you want. You may need a nice place to live, decent furniture, food, a vehicle, and some money to have fun with or provide for your children's future. Sometimes if you throw your petitions in the air, God catches them and sends down just enough to help you get by.

Likewise, if you help others with no conditions, whatever you need will come to you anyway. You may not attain power and fame, but you'll never be short of love, caring, and support. I'm no financial advisor, and God knows I've been down, but amazingly, when I was, I found out that at the tenement where I lived, everyone helped each other. We had potlucks and shared ideas on how to make

extra money, like organizing community garage
sales. I also called all my creditors and told them
I'd do my best to pay a small amount of what I
owed each month, and amazingly, they worked
with me. To this day, my kids remember those
times fondly.

(As an aside, avoidance and the "ostrich effect,"
or burying your head in the sand, are really risky
tactics, especially if you owe money to the IRS.
Phone your creditors, talk to them, and set up pay-
ments. If you're embarrassed or afraid, just remind
yourself that people are people. This technique
applies to all challenging situations, not just financial ones, because facing your fears head-on makes
your life more livable, even if it isn't pleasant. At
least you'll know where you stand, what goals you
need to set, and what you're working toward,
rather than staying stuck in that dark hole of fear
and apathy.)

Is the journey difficult at times? Yes, but you
just have to keep your eye on the doughnut instead
of on the hole. The attitude that says "What's the
use? I'll never get ahead anyway" is deadly, because
we become what we feel and think. On the flip side,
if you're going after fame and glory, be sure you
aren't deceiving yourself with false ego. It's often
better to be known by just a handful of people for

the right reasons than to be famous at the cost of your soul.

Can money buy you health? Love? Peace of mind? Of course not, but it helps when we have the resources to see the best doctors, to support a family, or pay the bills. We're told we should have retirement funds, college funds, life insurance, 401(k)s, investments, budgets, and on and on it goes, and we also have the age-old philosophy of "A penny saved is a penny earned." We just can't get too frugal and miserly and make money our God. Who hasn't heard of the poverty-stricken hermit who had millions hidden away, or the person who scrimped and saved to leave a fortune to a cat or a dog? (Now, being an animal lover, I can see providing for my pets, but how about leaving some of that money to an animal shelter, a game reserve, or the homeless?)

Even if your chart says that you're in for slim pickings, you can still modify or elongate the program you came in with. See yourself fulfilling your dreams, and ask for an abundance in whatever area you need it—but always with the condition that you'll share with others. I've seen this technique work time and again in my life. The money you give out will come back a hundredfold. After all, it isn't just the "bad" karma that returns to you; good karma is also your reward. The bottom line is, if you really embrace the philosophy that you're just renting your life and even your body, things flow so much easier!

Exercise

Divide a piece of paper in half. On the left, write what you *wish* you had, and on the right put what you *have now*. Below these columns, or on a second sheet of paper, make a list of all the things you really *need*. Now compare what you already have with your wants and needs. How much is truly required to survive?

When you've done the written exercise, take some time to look around at your home and think about what you actually enjoy or even notice. How many clothes do you wear, and how many of your possessions do nothing but gather dust? What items can you get rid of to make your life easier?

What I Wish I Had	What I Do Have
A new car	A great spouse
A bigger house	A home
A boat	A job that pays my bills

What I Need

Food

Shelter

Love

Clothing

Transportation

Affirmation

Each day, say to yourself: *"I go forward and leave the past as only a memory of what I have learned."*

Meditation

*Sit in a chair or lie in a prone position.
Take a deep breath and surround yourself
with white light, and around that put green
light. Now, in your mind, build yourself a
beautiful pink marble temple. Feel your
body completely relax as you construct
this pillared structure, which radiates with
light. Now take a deep breath, begin to
mount the marble steps, and as you ascend
them, say: "Every part of my body is in harmony with the universe. Even my organs
are in tune with God and my soul."*

*As you enter this edifice, you see that
the walls are decorated with murals. As
you look closer, you notice that these pictures are depictions of your life. It is as if
you are viewing the complete record of
your own life. First you see yourself as a
child, in both your happy and sad times. If
the face in the mural is sad, make it happy.
Walk a little farther and see yourself as a
teenager. This is the age you probably were
when you began to form ideas of what you
might do in your life. If you seem confused
or upset in any of these murals, again, blink*

and turn your countenance into one of contentment.

Next, see yourself in your 20s. Maybe at this point in your life you had a dream, but you got detoured. If so, add in the details of your story of how you got there. You are not changing your chart, you are simply fulfilling a desire of your soul's consciousness.

At the end of the long mural, you arrive at a blank wall. In this space, create a new image that illustrates what you need to accomplish to bring you abundance. Ask for God's help in showing you the road and finding the courage to take it. This path will be free of greed, and you will walk down it with the motto that everyone must win, and no one needs to get hurt. Each time you paint a scenario, a new solution to receiving abundance will come to you. You will know that nothing can stand in your way but you.

After you pass the murals, continue to walk through the temple until you reach what looks like an altar stone. Above the altar, a hologram appears, and you see yourself having enough to take care of *yourself and your loved ones. You feel younger, brighter, and full of purpose and passion. You no longer feel as if you are caught like a hamster on a wheel going very fast, but getting nowhere.*

Stay at the altar stone for a time, as long as you need to, and leave on it all the "could nots" "cannots" and "afraid to trys." Pick up the scepter of success and well-being, and when you are ready, turn around and walk out of this beautiful marble temple. As you descend the steps, you feel in control. You are not a victim of your life.

Finally, come out, all the way out . . . feeling better than you have ever felt before.

STEP 6

HOW TO FIND THE RIGHT RELATIONSHIP . . . AND ALSO LEARN TO BE ALONE

Over the 40-some years that I've been doing readings, the number-one, most-often-asked question has always remained the same:

"Where is Mr./Ms. Right?" There's nothing wrong with searching for a soul mate—in fact, it's very natural. Since the beginning of time, whether we believe in Adam and Eve or cavepeople, we've always lived in groups and paired off together (perhaps largely for protection). Even those of us who are loners by nature seek out partners—for example, nuns choose Christ as their mate when they take their vows. It's just an inherent part of being human. We're a species that was meant to be social, and of course, if we so choose, to procreate.

We all start out with some type of vision in our minds of what we think we want in a partner. This is what I like to call the "look, see, and love" or "lust" stage, when our hormones are in high gear—probably due to the fact that not so long ago, people had to get married and have children early because their life spans were much shorter. While it's no longer the case that we need to pair off at such a young age, our genetic wiring just hasn't caught up to our current time frame yet.

It's a shame that we don't learn this earlier, but the older we get, the more that companionship, trust, and communication take precedence over chemistry. Usually, a man or a woman at 21 is looking for something different from what a 60-year-old is. I'm not discouraging physical attraction—of course it's necessary, too—but for a lasting relationship, we should also try to engage our intellect.

Looking for Love

Before I get started on this topic, I want to offer a little disclaimer. Too often, we search for our "other half," not realizing that we have to be whole on our own, rather than waiting around for someone else to complete us. If we depend on other people to make us happy, we're definitely doomed to failure. In the same vein, there are many valid reasons to want a mate, but we must be careful not to neglect all the other marvelous relationships that we can have while we're here on Earth. From family to precious friends to animals, my life is filled with wonderful friendships that I'd never trade in just to say I had someone as my lover.

That being said, what should you be looking for in a relationship? Well, the good has to outweigh all other aspects; and this may surprise you, but the spirituality and beliefs of both partners is really key. Without that shared bond, there's nowhere to go and nothing to fall back on when life gives you the proverbial lemons.

You also have to be in a state of stability before you can find someone who will become welded to your soul. Begin by exploring who *you* are first, and then you'll have a clearer picture of what you need, as well as what you have to offer. For instance, if you're positive and upbeat, then someone who's cranky, jaded, and despondent wouldn't be an ideal mate to choose. (Otherwise, you may end up with the same types of people you've dated in the past; or you might simply follow your hormones, which we all know can make us blind, deaf, and dumb.) While it's very important that you make this list, for God's sake, make sure that you yourself live up to the standards you set for someone else. And whatever you do, don't go into a relationship thinking, *I can change this person.* You have to either accept people the way they are and love them, or move on.

There are certain places you can go to meet people that are better than others. For example, churches are a good spot to make contact, as are libraries and even grocery stores. Recently, a couple told me that they actually met at one of my book signings in Milwaukee and have been dating ever since. Seminars are great as well, because you'll most likely meet someone with common interests. I know that people say the Internet can be an easy way to get a date, but I think it's too dangerous. Not to mention that 90 percent of the time it's like trying to find love in a bar—a highly unlikely scenario, to say the least. Some dating services can be good, however, and these days, most of them put new members through a fairly thorough screening process, which is better than just running into someone in a seedy cocktail lounge.

You can't expect to find love if you lock yourself in a closet, but you also don't have to frantically search for a date everywhere you go or join every possible singles organization that's available. Energy attracts energy, and desperate energy will put anyone off. And when you meet someone, for heaven's sake, don't give them the litany of how you've been rejected and hurt—or almost as bad, how many boyfriends or girlfriends you've notched on your belt. Honesty may be the best policy, but who wants to hear a long, drawn-out sob story, or a rundown of your past conquests?

Ultimately, the best way to find a partner is to *stop looking so hard*. I know this may come as a surprise, but if you really want a relationship, then chances are 100 percent that you wrote one into your chart, otherwise you'd just prefer to be alone. If you just let go and let God handle everything, you'll meet someone when the time is right. Besides, let's say the worst-case scenario happens and you *don't* find anyone (which, by the way, I've rarely seen, but let's say it's destined)—do you spend the rest of your life in a state of despair and dejection? What a waste! Why not use that energy to form other relationships or work for society? You could help children and animals, spend more time with your friends and family, and make yourself the type of person whom others want to be around. Let's face it: A weeping, needy, dependent sap isn't even someone you'd want to invite to a party, let alone hang around with one-on-one.

Be in love with yourself, find your passion in caring for and helping others, and I guarantee that love will find you.

Avoiding Pitfalls

As I said at the beginning of this chapter, there's nothing wrong with chemistry—every successful relationship has it—but let's stop and think: Other than sex, what do you have in common with your lover? Do you both value understanding, compassion, communication, patience, trust, respect, and so on? Many times, if the physical attraction is strong, people make the age-old mistake of thinking, *I can change my partner.* I've heard it all before: "After we get married, he'll settle down,"or "Once we have a child, she'll become more responsible." The rule is, more often than not, these situations only get worse. Even if they just stay the same, is that really how you want to spend the rest of your life? As my grandmother used to say, "Ask yourself if you can stand this for 30, 40, or 50 years." If you think you can be happy with things as they are, great! If not, then that's when you know this is a relationship that isn't meant to be. And please know that *you can't change someone with an addiction,* whether it's to sex, drugs, or alcohol. You can help a person who's willing to go into therapy, but first he or she has to be ready to admit that there's a problem and decide to fix it.

There are many types of people you should flat-out avoid when you're looking for a partner. First are the *reflective personalities,* or folks who accuse you of the things they're actually guilty of. Then we have what I call the *lifeless-lump personalities.* These individuals can be very insidious, for initially, they seem to be your kindred soul, and like whatever you like. At the beginning it may be flattering that their world revolves around you, but it gets to be too much when you begin to feel that when you leave them, they stop existing. What seemed like a perfect match at the outset turns into a situation where you're basically performing like crazy to bring life into these tiring drips. These people are true parasites.

Then there are the *misogynists*—and even though this label by definition applies to men, trust me, there's a female version as well. These are the people who truly hate the opposite sex, so they try to lure you into psychological, emotional, or even physical abuse and wreak havoc with your life.

Then, right before you've finally had enough and decide to leave, these creeps do an about-face and for a time become very charming—that is, until they have you in their web again, and then they turn into their mean, vengeful old selves.

We also have the *undeveloped personalities,* who aren't too different from the lifeless lumps, except that they're far more immature. These are the folks who act helpless and can't seem to do anything on their own. Deep down, they're not only lazy, but they also have the prince or princess aura. In other words, they can't stand to get their hands dirty. They want all your attention all the time, and they demand that you wait on them, give them presents, and coddle them. If they don't get their way, they pout until someone gives in (isn't that endearing!).

Then we have the compulsive, jealous, *insecure personalities.* These individuals are always demanding to know where you've been and what you've been doing. It can be flattering for about a month or two, but then you start feeling strangled by their distrust and jealousy. I had a boyfriend like this years ago, and he'd constantly call to check in on me. Our conversations would go something like this:

"What are you doing?" he'd ask.

"Washing my hair," I'd reply.

"Why?"

"Because it's dirty."

"Are you sure you're not going out?"

"No, I'm just washing my hair," I'd repeat.

"At this time of night?"

"I didn't know there was a time frame on hair washing!"

"I saw that guy looking at you today," he'd counter.

"Yeah, so what?"

"Did you look back?"

"No," I'd respond.

"Yes, you did, I saw you."

As you can guess, this relationship didn't last long—it was just too exhausting and confining. Our last discussion eventually ended with my saying, "I'll see you around—and don't call me, I'll call you."

Last, we have my all-time favorites, the *sociopaths.* These are the true survivors of life—and not in a good way. Oh, they start off great, but soon turn to their dominating, manipulative selves. If they don't get their way, they'll leave you so fast that you won't know what hit you. They can replace you in a heartbeat. Trust me, even *I* have been involved with a sociopath, and I'm psychic, so don't feel bad if you fall prey to one, too.

Finally, please don't start a relationship with someone who's already married. These affairs can be the most defeating and the most doomed for failure, because rarely do the cheaters ever leave their partners. Even if they do, the third party, if he or she knowingly upsets a union, is in for some big-time karmic retribution. While I believe that no one can break up a truly happy marriage, does anyone really want to be the catalyst for broken hearts? Of course some people just like the ego boost they get from going after someone else's mate; it gives them a sense of power.

(I think it's worth mentioning here that you shouldn't waste your time longing after someone who's completely unavailable. For example, more often than you'd ever imagine, there are those who spend years pining over a celebrity, convinced that this famous person is for them. Yeah, right! And there are also people who just don't move on when someone says they're not interested. They think that if they keep trying, eventually the object of their "affection" will come around. Get real. Your time would be better spent cleaning out the garage or running some errands than wasting your days trying to figure out a way to make someone fall in love with you.)

Well, with all these bad eggs to sort through, you might think it's a wonder that anyone ever finds true love. But regardless of all the frogs, there still are princes and princesses out there. You just have to be willing to wait. And trust your instincts—if it drives you crazy that someone twiddles their thumbs or sucks their teeth (God help us), or even squeezes the toothpaste wrong, maybe these are only symptoms of a bigger problem. It doesn't necessarily mean that you can't put up with irritating habits—we all have them—but when you begin to look for anything and everything that's wrong and are ready to spring at the least provocation, maybe this person really isn't suited for you in a more fundamental sense.

Knowing When to Let Go

If you've ever been left by someone, rest assured that the law is that you'll find someone better. The same goes for ending a relationship as soon as you see that it's unhealthy. Don't stay with the wrong partner for too long, even though you know better, with the excuse, "But I love him/her." Well, as hard as it may be for you to face, your partner doesn't love you, or else you wouldn't have been left broken and bleeding.

The other thing you don't want to do is stay in a relationship because you're afraid to be alone, or because of economic reasons. This is really foolish. As far as money goes, there's always something you can be trained to do, and most states have community-property laws. Besides, what price are you willing to put on your health and happiness, or the well-being of your children?

Even though I'm going to talk about this in the next chapter in more detail, I need to briefly address divorce and death at this point. In many ways, the two are very similar—they represent a change of lifestyle. What you knew and felt secure about is no longer there, and filling the void is excruciating grief. Death takes away the person you lived with and trusted, as does divorce. While there are divorces that are amicable, and some people simply outgrow each other, there are many cases where a faithful spouse is abandoned for a moment of lust and self-gratification. This can really kill your trust in others and shatter all you believe in. No matter what the scenario is, divorce can leave both partners feeling out of sync, to say the least.

I recommend that before you file for divorce, you try *everything*—especially counseling, where you take time out to honestly talk to each other. After all, the one thing that brings down more relationships than any other issue is when people stop communicating. When you first met your lover, you were probably enamored with him or her, and you could talk for hours. But over time, life crawled in and you may have gotten bored. This happens especially when you don't keep your mind open to discussing things, and instead settle down in a humdrum survival mode where you no longer show interest in what your partner has to say. Then, before long, the two of you begin to live lives of quiet desperation, and it's all over.

The best way to handle death or divorce is to get over it as fast as you can. The death of a loved one is terribly heartbreaking, but at least you're not left with the feeling that you were rejected for another person. And even though it may not be comforting at first, there's some solace in the knowledge that you will be reunited on the Other Side. Death, although painful, is natural, while divorce, I'm convinced, is unnatural. I don't mean to imply that there aren't times when it's definitely warranted, but it always leaves you with the feeling that you weren't good enough on some level. Just remember that as long as you don't crawl into a hole, God will come in and make your life well again, and you'll be able to enjoy another day.

All of life is a test, as you've heard me say so many times, and as dark as it gets, there *will* be daylight again if you try to get out there and be positive. You'll adjust, and you'll feel better knowing that you've successfully made it through another lesson.

Exercise

In your journal or on a blank piece of paper, make a two-column list. On the left, write out what you don't want in a partner, and on the right, put what you do want. Be honest: You might be surprised that the type of person you want today isn't the same as what you were looking for several years ago. Life and its experiences somehow change our outlook and perspective.

<u>What I Don't Want in a Partner</u>	<u>What I Want in a Partner</u>
A self-centered individual	Someone who's spiritual and kind
A workaholic	Someone who enjoys the outdoors
A person who's always jealous	Someone trustworthy

Now, on another page, make a second chart. On the left side, list the qualities you don't like about yourself—the things you want to change. On the right, put down what you *do* like about yourself. Review both sides every day this week, and watch how you not only change, but the world around you improves, too.

<u>Things about Myself I'd Like to Change</u>	<u>Things about Myself I Like</u>
I'd like to be more careful with money.	I'm a wonderful gardener.

I'm going to try to be less judgmental.	I treat my family and friends with love and respect.
I want to develop more patience.	I'm a good problem solver.

Affirmation

This week, look in a mirror as you say the following: *"I do not fear success or failure, because in success I learn control, and in failure I learn to try again."*

Meditation

As before, sit or lie down in a prone position. Start breathing deeply from your diaphragm, and when you exhale, say, "I am releasing all desperation and negativity, all feelings of unworthiness and rejection. I am energized in the mind and creative force of God, and I deserve to love and be loved."

Relax your whole body, beginning with your feet, ankles, calves, thighs, and pelvic girdle; and continue all the way up through the trunk of your body, your spine, neck, arms, hands, and head area. Say, "From the top of my head to my toes, I am one complete unit, able to love, survive, and sustain my life in the glory of God." See yourself as brighter, younger, better looking, more intelligent, and with a positive attitude.

Now visualize yourself in a crowd of people. Push your energy out so that you create what we call "presence." Say, "I am created by God to make a difference, so I walk with the white light of the Holy Spirit around me. I release all past mistakes, rejections, and embarrassments, and I will not repeat them in the future. I learn to laugh at myself."

Now visualize yourself in a beautiful meadow. It looks like it has just rained, because the grass is lush and the foliage is green. You look up and see a rainbow, and you run over and stand in its light. You can see the colors on your body—the green for healing, the gold for higher power, the blue for peace and tranquility, and the reddish-pink for love. The hues infiltrate every part of your being. Now say, "I am in the state of loving, and I am ready for love to come to me."

Now bring yourself out of this relaxed state, all the way out, feeling marvelous, energized, and better than you have in a long, long time.

STEP 7

HOW TO DEAL WITH THE DEATH OF A LOVED ONE AS WELL AS THE PAIN OF DIVORCE

In my book *A Journal of Love and Healing* (Hay House, 2001), which I wrote with Nancy Dufresne, I invite you on a journey through my personal losses, and provide you with space to record your own thoughts and feelings about the grief you may have experienced in your life. In *this* book, however, I want to specifically address steps that you can take to get through the difficult times.

The pain you feel when you lose a loved one, whether through death or divorce, is like a dragon in your gut that wants to devour you—and you know you can't escape it. Be patient with yourself when you're mourning, because everyone goes through grief in stages. Even when the person you love is sick for a long time and you know the inevitable outcome, you'll still experience denial when death finally arrives. Then, after you've gotten over your disbelief, the "robot" stage can set in. When this happens, you'll know that you're moving and breathing, but you'll be completely disconnected from everything going on around you. Your primal instincts will kick in and take over, and you'll just go on autopilot. During this complete collapse of mind, body, and spirit, chances are that no one will be able to reach you.

Again, whether you're going through a divorce or facing the death of someone you love, there isn't any easy way to overcome the sadness of a loss. Those of us who have been through it know that there are many things in life you can ignore or escape, but this isn't one of them. However, if you can manage to smile through your tears, then one day you'll awaken from this long trial. And although you'll bear certain scars for the rest of your life, you *will* smile and even laugh again. Then, when the pain returns, as it will from time to time, you can comfort yourself with the knowledge that you've survived life's most difficult challenge.

The Death of a Loved One

Everyone's grief is relative to them—just as happiness is. I don't like to quantify pain, but I feel that the death of a child is by far the most tragic loss one can go through. This doesn't minimize the anguish you may feel when a parent, spouse, or friend passes away, since these are all life-altering events, but to lose a child is beyond comparison.

Yet even though death may seem unfair—and for those who are left behind, it certainly leaves a deep wound—it's a part of life that's as natural as eating or sleeping. In fact, the end is really the beginning for all of us, since our true Home is on the Other Side. I know that this may not be much comfort when we're still caught here in "hell" (and this life *is* hell in the sense that we're here to learn some difficult lessons), but our friends and family members who have passed over are all happy where they are!

I lost two more loved ones this past year, one of them being Abass Nadim, who was my Egyptian tour guide and dearest friend. He died of a heart attack while vacationing in Peru. First of all, I told him not to go on this trip, and warned him that if he did, he should not go climbing. He did both. I've been asked if I have the power to control other people's lives, and while of course I can't, I sometimes wish I could. I loved Abass, and even though he contacted me just after his death to tell me he was okay, I was still shocked and angry that this wondrous light went out of so many lives. A million memories filled my mind: his love of life and his children, the times we laughed, and how he would call to cheer me up when I was going through a painful divorce. *How will Egypt be the same without him?* I wondered. I went through the normal stages of disbelief and shock, and then I remembered that this life is like a dream, and one day, we'll all wake up and be with our loved ones again.

Similarly, just a week before he passed away, I'd expressed to my friend Kevyn Aucoin, the celebrity makeup artist, that I was worried about him. He just laughed it off. I won't go into the details, but soon after, a beautiful, talented soul was lost to us. Kevyn gave me a message after he left this world, saying, "I'm sorry that I didn't plant the flowers." (Later, his family validated that he had been meaning to get some flowers planted.) Still, once again, I was left with that hollow ache and the often-asked question, "Why him?" When you see so many dark, evil entities living out their lives and blithely making everyone miserable, it's almost impossible to understand why the gentle, caring ones among us are often taken so suddenly.

It may be difficult to comprehend, but there's a reason why good people take their exit points early and cross over to the Other Side. You see, we each have five exit points that we can take to go Home. Many times, the most kindhearted people take them early because they're tired of life, they feel that they've completed their mission for God, and they're simply ready to go. When I was 26 and had my near-death experience, I was told by a beautiful entity to go back to Earth because I had more to do. I could also faintly hear a nurse screaming, "Don't go, Sylvia, we need you!" What really drew me back, however, was the fact that for a split second it entered my consciousness that I didn't want to leave my only son (at the time), Paul, with my first husband.

If you haven't ever believed in an afterlife, I can only tell you that I've received thousands of e-mails and letters from people who have visited the Other Side in dreams, astral travels, near-death experiences, and hypnosis regressions, and they all describe the same topographical features. (I discuss the geography of the Other Side in more detail in my book *The Other Side and Back*.) How can these people from different religions, cultures, and ethnic groups—both skeptics and believers alike—all see the same thing? Statistically it's an impossibility; and from the perspective of a researcher, when you keep running into identical accounts, you not only believe, you have confirmation. Personally, I'm convinced that our souls not only survive death, but they go to a place of beauty and peace where we're all reunited with our loved ones who have passed before us.

This brings us to another important question: Why do some people make it to the Other Side, while others don't? In other words, how do we explain ghosts and hauntings? It's compelling that so many of us are interested in ghosts, considering that out of all the people who have ever died, these entities make up a very small percentage. Perhaps it's because these beings offer evidence that *something* exists beyond this life. The truth is that a ghost is the restless soul of a person who had unfinished business or an unresolved conflict here on Earth or suffered a traumatic death and wasn't ready to die. (By the way, I'm continually amazed that almost all religions teach that the soul survives, but if you say that you've seen a ghost, everyone gets suspicious or afraid. Why should we, as spiritual psychics, put up with these skeptics? Why don't the naysayers follow around religious people and put down *their* belief system, which like ours, is rooted in the belief in a God that doesn't abandon us and a soul that survives?)

All loved ones can show up in dreams or send us messages in our waking hours, but this doesn't mean that they're ghosts. Those who have gone to the Other Side can communicate with us by leaving a scent, such as roses or cigarette smoke; dropping coins; ringing phones; and making electrical devices turn off and on. Animals and children especially can see loved ones who have passed over, and I'm convinced it's because of their innocence—that is, no one has told them they *can't* see these visitors. Again, hauntings are much different, because they give us a bad feeling, cause bizarre things to happen, and don't stop. Once souls make the transition to the Other Side, it really becomes difficult for them to get into this dense atmosphere and manifest themselves, but they do come in times of great stress or need, especially in our dreams.

As a medium, the most important thing I do is to assure those who are left behind that their loved one made it to the Other Side. Yes, it's validating to be able to give information about how a person died or where they stashed a sentimental piece of jewelry before they went (as I'm sometimes asked), but I'm most gratified when I get the message that another soul has graduated and made the transition.

In all the regressions I've done (a regression is when I guide someone back in time to a past-life memory while they're in a hypnotic state), I've never come across anyone who remembers having a bad death experience. All my ministers who do regressions, primarily to release past-life traumas and show us where we are in the scope of our development for God, have also reported the same thing—it doesn't seem as if there are any bad death experiences. Of course, horrendous things may happen to someone just before death, such as torture, and they may be frustrated that they were killed unjustly, but when the tunnel opens, there's only peace and joy.

On the other hand, I've also taken people through the birth experience in a regression, and *this* is where you really get into pain, suffering, and trauma. I'm convinced that we spend our whole lives never truly getting over leaving Home and going through the ordeal of birth, which in my belief is the true death. Honestly, there were times when it was so painful to watch a person go through the birth experience that I either had to stop the regression completely or put the individual in an observant position so he or she didn't have to go through it all over again (it's standard practice for any professional, authentic hypnotist doing regression to put their client in an observant position when things get too horrifying). The bottom line is that these regressions prove that we have it all backward—we're coming from heaven to hell, and when we leave this planet, we go back Home to paradise.

It also stands to reason that no matter how bad it gets here on Earth, most of us don't really want to leave, because we've made it our home for so many years and have formed loving relationships here. I even get teary when I leave my grandchildren to go on the road to do book tours and seminars. I know that I'm coming back, but I miss them while I'm gone. It's even more difficult to say good-bye to people we might not see for months, years, or ever again. Think of times of war, when wives, husbands, lovers, mothers, fathers, and siblings have had to bid each other farewell, some never to see each other again in this life.

I just read a book about Abigail Adams (John Adams's wife) entitled *Dearest Friend* (by Lynne Withey). In it, Abigail records in her journal the longing and loneliness she feels when her husband is away fulfilling his political duties, while she's left alone to raise her children and run the farm. There was even a five-year period in which she saw him only once. Just as the hope of an eventual reunion kept this First Lady going during those long, lonely years, we too can rest assured that we will see our loved ones again. Death isn't the end; it's like a trip that we'll all go on, and some of us just take an earlier train.

Divorce

Divorce can cause a pain that's very similar to death. Actually, I've had many people tell me that dealing with death can be easier than going through a divorce. Having experienced both, I can say that although they're different ordeals, they're very similar with respect to the fact that they both change lives forever. Unfortunately, when a marriage is dissolved, however, people don't usually offer you the same sympathy that you get when someone you love dies, and this can compound any feelings of failure or isolation that you may have.

As I've already mentioned, divorces often come about because one of the spouses has found someone else. In other cases, there is abuse or just a breakdown in communication. In the situations where infidelity is the cause of the breakup, the party who is pursuing a relationship may feel torn by guilt, while the other person is left with the horrible feeling of rejection, as if they've failed because they weren't good enough. In a divorce, no one really wins, especially if children are involved.

Like most of us, there was a time in my life when I dreamed of getting married, having children, and staying with one person for the rest of my life. It didn't work out that way because of abuse. (Although even then, I wanted to stay in my marriage, especially since in my family, divorce was unheard of. But when I considered the well-being of my children, I knew that I had no other choice.) Anxiety, fear, and the unfamiliar lifestyle of raising my kids alone was overwhelming at times, but I did learn from my divorce. Ultimately, I just had to throw myself back into my work, my family, my belief system, and my friends, and day by day, life brightened up.

All grief, mine and yours, can be called selfish. I don't really care what you call it; it's still a void, and we have every right to feel sorry for ourselves and mourn our loss. It's aggravating beyond words when someone asks you if you're "over it yet." It makes me want to scream, "No! And you know what? I never, ever will be!" A song, a taste, a smell, a phrase, places, pictures—any of these can trigger the emotions that are lying behind the thin membrane called "survival."

The reality is that none of us knows when the loss of a loved one will turn our world upside down. So, in the meantime, the best we can do is simply hold on to each moment we have, and remember to tell our family and friends how much we love them. We have the present, this instant in time, and like money, we can either savor and enjoy it or spend it frivolously and end up with nothing to show for it. Every day I make it a point to hold my loved ones a little closer than I did the day before, and I rest easy knowing that they will always be with me.

Exercise: Death of a Loved One

Again, either in your journal or on a blank piece of paper, make two columns. On the left, write down what it is you loved most about the person you lost. On the right side of the paper, write down what you wish you could have said or done before the person passed away.

What I Loved Most	What I Wish I Could Have Said or Done
Her jokes and smiles	I wish I would have been more of a companion.
Her selfless nature	I wish I could have taken her on the trip I always promised.
Her hugs	I wish I could have spent more time with her before she got sick.

Read through the right side of the column again. Have you been carrying around a lot of unnecessary guilt? If so, know that you've started to release these feelings by writing them down here.

Exercise: Divorce

Take out a sheet of paper or turn to a blank page in your journal. On the left side of the paper, write down what you feel you could have done differently, which might have prevented your divorce. On the right side, make a list of all the positive qualities you did bring to the relationship.

What I Could Have Done Differently	What I Did Bring to the Relationship
I could have complained less about our finances.	I did try to listen.
I could have spent more time with my spouse.	I was truly caring.
I could have agreed to go to counseling sooner.	I always supported my spouse's career.

Look back at your lists. You'll see that the left side is also the "guilt" side, and the right side represents all the strong points you still possess. Learn from the guilt, but then let it go.

Affirmation

Every day this week, say to yourself: "*I do not push against life; instead, I let God and my chart guide me. I measure my life by my motives when I fear that I have done wrong things, and I realize that I did not mean to hurt anyone.*"

Meditation for the Death of Your Loved Ones

Lie down in a comfortable position. Relax your body, starting with your toes and going upward through your feet, ankles, calves, thighs, pelvic girdle, trunk, arms, hands, shoulders, neck, and head— just as you have done in the other meditations. Let your breathing become rhythmic, as if you are falling asleep. Now close your eyes, and imagine yourself up above your body.

Instead of pushing your grief away and burying it in your body, let it boil up and come out. It is like giving birth, only you don't have to be brave and grit your teeth; you can just let yourself go. Let the montage of memories fill your mind, and feel the pain or joy or whatever emotions come your way. If you feel regret or guilt creep in, know that these emotions were part of a lesson learned, but you don't need them anymore.

See yourself going through the tunnel (you will not die) and embracing your loved ones. If you keep doing this, they will give you a telepathic message. Regardless of what validation you want or get, be aware that they made it to the Other Side, which is Home, and they are happy and you will one day be with them. Say to yourself, "I will talk to my loved ones and keep them alive in my memories and thoughts. I know that my loved ones will never leave me, and this gives me solace."

If you would like to, take a walk in a meadow or a rose garden with your loved ones. See their happy, smiling faces and know they have not forgotten you. Feel their presence and their touch. It is all so real that you can even smell them. Your pain begins to flow out of you as your blessed angels surround you with their healing wings of protection. Feel your spirit guide standing by you as a helpful companion. Feel the light of the Holy Spirit fill your heart with grace, hope, and conviction, and know that you will only be separated from your loved ones for a short time, and you will see them again after you finish your schooling. Ask your loved ones for a sign. Ask them to come to you not only in the meditative state, but in your dreams as well. Perhaps, with God's help, you can go out of your body astrally and meet them on the Other Side.

Do not block grief, but know beyond any doubt that your loved ones want you to go on with your life. To fall down and not get up is no way to celebrate the life of someone who was taken from you. Make a concerted effort to not only love again (although perhaps not ever in the same way), but to help others who are in pain and loss.

Bring yourself back now, all the way back to complete consciousness, feeling lighter in your heart and soul and knowing that your loved ones are happy and finally Home.

Meditation for Divorce

Put yourself in a comfortable position. Again, relax yourself by going from your toes to your head, relaxing each part of your body along the way. Breathe deeply from the diaphragm and ask that all the hurts and rejections be put into a tiny ball of pain and sent away. Exhale, and as you do so, blow this little ball up, up, and away from you.

Surround yourself with pink light, which represents love. Know that you will love and be loved again. Let go of all the "should haves" and "could haves." Open your hands and let the hurt and vengeance be released. Also, surround your former partner with both pink and white light so that neither of you keeps absorbing the other's negativity.

See yourself alone on a road. At first you are a little frightened, as it seems to go nowhere, but you force yourself to walk. All of a sudden, the air gets lighter, the sun is warm, and there is a breeze that gently blows your hair. Now you are aware of the beautiful rolling hills and the array of flowers along the way. You, a complete, capable human being, can walk this road. Your step is lighter and your mind and heart are clear, as if a weight has been lifted. You wish yourself and your former partner health, happiness, and a sense of peace, and you close this one chapter in the very long book that is your chart. You will live to love another day.

Bring yourself back now, back to complete consciousness, feeling lightened by the release of pain and negativity, and realizing that there is a new world awaiting you—a world in which love will find its way to you.

STEP 8

HOW TO KEEP YOURSELF IN A STATE OF WELLNESS AND AVOID GETTING SICK

Wherever we go these days, it seems that we're bombarded by conflicting information about health. Practically every week there's a new study published about what causes cancer, what helps combat cholesterol, and how we can improve our circulation. Then we're told that we need to exercise, but we're warned that if we exert ourselves too much, we could blow out our knees and wrench our backs. Well, the great thing about research is that the more you investigate something, the more you discover and the more you learn. In this chapter, I've done my best to sort through the confusion and provide you with a solid plan to stay in top shape—both physically and mentally.

Establishing a Healthy Diet

Let's start with the basics. I know that I'm going to fly in the face of some vegetarians here, but after 50 years of research in wellness (not medicine), I can tell you that sugar is truly, without a doubt, very lethal to your system. And what most people don't realize is that everything that isn't protein is sugar! Now God knows that I love animals, but if we weren't meant to consume meat, we wouldn't have canine teeth, we'd only have flat teeth. Besides, what vegetarians don't realize is that when you cut a plant, it screams.

I really don't care what form your protein comes in, but you'd better stock up on it because it's the primary building block of your cells, and you can't feed a bunch of sugar to a protein organism and not expect the cells to crumble. Does that mean I believe you have to walk around with a big fat piece of meat sticking out of your mouth all day? God, no! I'm not a big fan of red meat because it makes me feel too full and lethargic, but chicken, fish, turkey, eggs, legumes, beans, and the like are all good sources of protein.

Every time I've told someone who has an immune-deficiency illness such as fibromyalgia, chronic fatigue syndrome, and even AIDS to go on a high-protein diet, their body immediately responds positively. Not only that, but it helps these people achieve a healthy weight. Even diabetics should be on this type of diet. After all, how in God's name can a diabetic eat a ton of sugar—and that includes salads, fruits, vegetables, starches, and so on—and not affect his or her health? The same goes for everyone: If you keep your carbohydrate intake low, you'll not only feel better, but your immune system will pick up as well.

People will say, "But doesn't a high-protein diet hurt your kidneys?" The answer is no, because you're not just going to eat fatty meat, but chicken and fish, and you'll drink lots of water. However, be sure to avoid ingesting too many dairy products, because these can cause problems (because of the lactose). The real key is moderation. Let's face it: Too many diet sodas may not cause you to gain weight, but they sure can ravage your kidneys and bladder, not to mention that the caffeine intake can make you wired.

As far as supplements go, take a multivitamin with all the recommended daily vitamins and minerals. Actually, prenatal vitamins work great for a lot of people—not just expectant women. They can even help keep your hair from falling out, believe it or not! Then, as a little extra insurance, invest in an amino-acid complex and pop three of those a day—morning, afternoon, and evening.

The most important thing you can do for your health is to listen to your body. If you feel bloated after you eat asparagus, then don't keep eating it. If radishes upset your digestion, avoid them—your body is telling you that this food isn't right for you. We've all heard people say, "I'm eating this now because I love it, but I'll sure pay for it tomorrow!" If you're stupid enough to keep doing something that hurts you, just imagine what your insides are going through. And bear in mind that when your body is ill, your brain suffers, too. When you don't feel well, you can't think, and you can't perform at your highest level.

This is precisely why I can't understand why people abuse drugs or alcohol. You're going to be sorry, not just in the next few days, but further down the road for what you do to your body today. How can one evening of pleasure be worth the sickness, guilt, and grief that follows? Sure, some people claim that these substances help them relax, but relaxation isn't six or eight hours of being stupid, silly, or numb. Besides, if you get drunk or high, you're just adding more problems to the heap of stress that you were trying to escape from in the first place. And not only are you literally killing brain cells by the thousands, you're also ensuring that your liver and pancreas begin to look like Swiss cheese. You may be able to get away with it now, but trust me, you'll pay the piper one day.

Dealing with Stress

In this day and age, unless you're a complete couch potato, you're probably very familiar with stress. Stress doesn't just cause mental anguish, it can take a physical toll as well. The problem really begins when you get caught up in just one focus, such as a relationship with a family member, a financial problem, or a challenging situation at work, and you feel that you have no form of escape. When this happens, you need to take your mind out of the groove of your immediate concern and put your energy into something else, such as painting, exercise, writing, or whatever. If you can't change gears in your own mind, there isn't any vacation you can go on or any spa treatment you can enjoy that will refocus you and free you of your anxiety.

Some people tell me, "Well, I don't have a hobby, I just work." That makes me want to scream, "Have you tried?!" Make an effort to get passionate about other things. Personally, instead of just "going flat" or becoming incapacitated in response to a stressful situation, I'll do needlepoint, write, walk, garden, or play with my grandchildren. You can take a night course once a week at a community college to learn another language, Feng Shui, philosophy, or even real estate—anything that gives that one sector of your brain some relief.

Think of your mind as a busy office: Some parts answer phones, some make appointments, and some handle the distribution of outgoing products. But if your routine is the same day in and day out, your mind will eventually go numb for lack of stimulation. To prevent this, try doing what I do in my office: I actually have my employees learn others' jobs and rotate periodically. After all, show me someone who "blanks" his or her mind, going through the day without actually thinking and being challenged, and I'll show you an android.

Obviously, I'm also a believer in the power of meditation to change your focus and sharpen your mind. It's a pursuit that can be active, rewarding, and relaxing, and it's also very good for affirming your goals. Many athletes I know will meditate and see themselves achieving an objective, whether it's winning a race, skating with more precision than ever, or hitting a home run. I can't say this enough: As the mind visualizes, the body follows suit.

There's a theory that I've found to be more true than false: When people get sick—even terminally ill—and they change their lifestyle, job, or other stress-related factors, they often get better. Follow this advice, and at the very least, you'll have a healthier, happier day.

Learning from Our Cell Memory

Sometimes it isn't just the stress of *this* life that affects your health. In some of my other books, especially *Past Lives, Future Healing* (New American Library, 2002), I've addressed how we carry cell memories over from past lives into this one. As a brief example, if you were hung in another life, then today you might avoid tight clothes and choker necklaces. Likewise, if you drowned, you could have a fear of deep water, because your cells, whether you know it or not, can carry memories from one life to the next. Sometimes, as I mentioned in Step 3, these behaviors and phobias don't appear until you reach the same age that you were when the trauma occurred in a past life.

I've also explained that birthmarks, more often than not, can be scars or reminders of our past lives. For instance, I know of a woman with a brown birthmark on her back who was shot with an arrow when she was a Cherokee in a past life. Now in this life, not only does she not want anyone to sneak up behind her, but she often experiences inexplicable pain in that area.

Why is this important to know? Well, because as I said in Step 3, if we can release the fears we have left over from past lives and realize that we're safe today, we can eliminate the physical and mental symptoms that these memories cause. Of course I don't mean to give the impression that we should just assume that every ache and pain is the result of past-life trauma. We should always, *always* see our physician and get everything checked when we sense that something is out of sync. And yes, I *do* believe in holistic and alternative therapies, but as I tell all my clients, who wants to treat a hot, inflamed gallbladder with grape-seed extract?! Thank God we also have access to modern medicine. (Then again, on the other side of the coin, I'm getting a little fed up with all the TV advertisements for pharmaceuticals. I know some folks who take so many pills that they don't even remember what they're all for. There has to some middle ground.)

Don't Get Drained

Aside from cell memory, mistreating your body, and stressing out about things you can't change, the one thing I really want to impress upon you is that it's not just situations that make us sick, but people. This may come as a surprise, but think about it: Our interactions with other individuals make up our lives, so of course they affect us! Does that mean we should run away to a convent or monastery to avoid being influenced by our friends, family members, co-workers, and even perfect strangers? We could, but it's really not necessary as long as we just make a point of being aware of how other people affect us. It takes a little introspection and detective work, but trust me, you can do it.

During my first marriage, before I was aware of this phenomenon, I'd wake up every morning feeling exhausted. One night my husband was sick, so I slept alone. To my surprise, the next day I woke up very refreshed. Then, when I tried sleeping with him again, I woke up drained. So to confirm my suspicions, I tried going to bed alone a second time, and sure enough, I felt better. I realized then that people can drain you while you sleep, just as they can sap your energy in any unguarded moment. (This doesn't mean that I recommend that married people sleep alone; I'm simply pointing out that we all need to be aware of people and situations that sap our vitality.)

You don't have to be asleep for someone to leech off your life force either. I used to spend a lot of time with a certain friend whom I really cared about, but after spending an hour with her, I felt as if the blood had been drained from my body. Does this mean that she was a bad person? Not necessarily. More often than not, these folks are just self-centered. They're exhausting because you find yourself constantly having to give out your energy to make them feel better.

Perhaps the solution to this problem is as simple as a little honesty, both with yourself and the person you're interacting with. After all, how often do you tell people how you feel? You don't have to be cruel, but sometimes friendships and love affairs are too expensive to hold on to at any cost. When they cause you excessive stress, time, and energy, maybe it's time to ask yourself if they're really worth the price you're paying.

First impressions are more accurate than most people imagine, but we're taught otherwise and that's wrong. The more you listen to your first impressions, the more powerful your psychic ability becomes. I mean, how many times have you said, "I don't feel right about this person," and later found out that you were right to be wary? This week, try trusting your instincts. When you meet new people, feel and sense how they affect you. Let your internal psychic antenna work for you. Do you like them? Do they repel you? Or do you just feel nothing? If you really enjoy being around them, this means that they're on the same wavelength that you're on, and chances are you'll rejuvenate each other. If you get an immediate bad vibe, they could be dark inside, or just totally off your energy wave. It doesn't matter which it is, just move on. If you feel completely neutral, then a close friendship probably wouldn't be of much benefit to either of you, and it may be the case that you'd just bore each other, so there's no point in putting a lot of energy into a relationship.

People sometimes ask me what they should do if a family member is the one draining their energy. Well, as strange as this may seem, you have to distance yourself from them. You don't have to offend anyone, just quietly make yourself absent from their presence when you can help it, and when you do have to see them, visualize yourself surrounded by white light and make your visit short and sweet. (Children, as pure as they are, can be draining, but it isn't their fault. Usually we find ourselves zapped of energy when we're around them because *we're* overdoing it.)

If you feel sick, look around you. Do all the right things medically and physically, but also look to see whom you're with. Then be honest with yourself and move on. If you put out a spiritual, giving vibration, then the right people will soon come to you.

Exercise

There are three parts to this exercise, so you'll need a few blank pieces of paper or a few pages in your journal. Divide the three sheets of paper into two columns. On the first page, call the left column "Stressful Situations," and in it, list all the events and circumstances that really stress you out. On the right, label the column "Feel-Good Situations," and write all the things that make you feel relaxed and happy. See the example that follows.

Stressful Situations	Feel-Good Situations
Deadlines at work	Singing
Traffic	Going to the movies
Paying bills	Eating dinner with my family

Study the left side carefully. Can you eliminate any of these factors? Remember, this is your *life*—how important is good health and happiness? If there are situations that you truly can't avoid, then find something from your list on the right that you can do that will at least give you some relief (such as singing along to the radio when you're stuck in rush-hour gridlock). Change your focus, and be passionate about the things you love to do!

Now, in the left-hand column on the second piece of paper, make a list of all the negative things you do to your body. On the right, jot down the things you know you could do to feel better and improve your physical health. Again, see the example on the next page.

Negative Things I Do to My Body	What I Can Do to Nurture My Body
Drinking too much	Exercise three times a week
Eating out too often	Drink more water
Not getting enough sleep	Take a relaxing bath

Study both lists. You know what you need to do to treat your body better!

On the last sheet of paper, write down all the people who irritate you or drain you on the left, and on the other side, put all the people who make you feel good. Your list could look something like this:

People Who Drain/Irritate Me	People Who Make Me Feel Good
My uncle	My granddaughter
My co-worker	My spouse
Telemarketers	My neighbor

Try to stay away from the people on the left—even if they're family members. If you have to see them, try to make your visits short. Spend time with the people you listed on the right-hand side as much as possible, and you'll find yourself becoming a happier person.

Affirmation

Take a moment every day this week to say to yourself: *"I am the master of my life and my chart, and no one can take this away from me. I succeed and stay on track."*

Meditation

Begin by surrounding yourself with emerald-green light This color represents healing. Once you've done so, relax yourself as you have in the other meditations, but since this one is geared toward your mental, physical, and spiritual health, be even more meticulous. Starting with your toes, slowly relax and unstress each foot, instep, and ankle, and then move a green healing light up your calves, thighs, and pelvic girdle. At any point in your body where you experience pain, pause and layer it with extra green light. [Again, the exercises in this book are not intended to replace a visit to your physician.] *Keep moving this sparkling green light up through the trunk of your body, threading through all the organs therein. Now move up your neck and down your shoulders, into your upper arms, lower arms, hands, and fingertips. Bring the light up through your face and head area, and ask that your intellect and emotion be cemented together.*

Request that any emotion that's causing pain be controlled by your intellect—the executive, God-given I Am. Call upon the Archangels with their green healing wands to come and encircle you and place their wings and wands on all aggravated or sick areas. [The Archangels are the healers of the angels.]

See yourself standing in a flowing garment, looking at a tall mountain. You begin to climb the mountain, and to your surprise, the ascent is effortless and you feel full of life and health. The mountain is grassy and the breeze is gently blowing as you reach the top. At the summit, pause and look around at the beautiful vista. Sit there for a while, feeling at peace with no pain or depression—only beauty and calm and a sense of being in control of your mind, body, and spirit. This is the time to make a resolution to heal yourself. If you want to, also resolve not to do anything that would be toxic for you. Take a deep breath and feel your body let go of pain, anxiety, and depression, whether from this or any past life.

Now as you look down, you begin to see all the people who are part of your life circulating below you. Watch them very closely. Do you want them up on top with you, or do you want to leave them below? One by one, call the ones you want with you to come up and share your space. You may be surprised at this point—there may be some people you really don't want with you anymore because you have come a long way in your spiritual understanding.

Sit at the top of the mountain for as long as you would like, feeling healthier and younger and more vibrant than ever before.

Eventually bring yourself down from the grassy peak and repeat to yourself, "I am with God, the true Guardian of the temple of my body."

Bring yourself back into consciousness with that green light whirling around you, all the way up, on the count of three . . . one, two, three.

AFTERWORD

If you're diligent about reading and studying the information and exercises offered in this book— even though you might not always agree with everything I say—I guarantee that it will make you continue to think, and will deepen your search. You just may come to the same conclusions that I have.

Regardless, as Jesus said, "Ask, and it shall be given to you; seek, and ye shall find; knock, and it shall be opened unto you." Isn't that truly the purpose of life? To learn about and elevate our souls for God?

God love you . . . I do!

— **Sylvia**

ABOUT THE AUTHOR

Millions of people have witnessed **Sylvia Browne's** incredible psychic powers on TV shows such as *Montel, Larry King Live,* *Entertainment Tonight,* and *Unsolved Mysteries,* and she has been profiled in *Cosmopolitan* and *People* magazines and other national media. Sylvia is the author of numerous books and audios; is president of the Sylvia Browne Corporation; and is the founder of her church, the Society of Novus Spiritus, located in Campbell, California.

Please contact Sylvia at: **www.sylvia.org,** or call **(408) 379-7070** for further information about her work.

NOTES

NOTES

NOTES
➳✛⬳

NOTES

HAY HOUSE TITLES OF RELATED INTEREST

BOOKS

After Life: Answers from the Other Side, by John Edward

Caroline Myss' Journal of Inner Dialogue:
Working with Chakras, Archetypes,
and Sacred Contracts, by Caroline Myss

Meditations to Heal Your Life, by Louise L. Hay

Mirrors of Time:
Using Regression for Physical, Emotional, and Spiritual
Healing (book-with-CD), by Brian L. Weiss, M.D.

Soul Coaching:
28 Days to Discover Your Authentic Self, by Denise Linn

Turning Inward:
A Journal of Self-Reflection, by Cheryl Richardson

CARD DECKS

Healing Cards, by Caroline Myss and Peter Occhiogrosso

Healing the Mind and Spirit Cards,
by Brian L. Weiss, M.D.

Messages from Your Angels Cards, by Doreen Virtue, Ph.D.

Miracle Cards, by Marianne Williamson

Until Today Cards, by Iyanla Vanzant

All of the above are available at your local bookstore,
or may be ordered through Hay House, Inc.

We hope you enjoyed this Hay House book.
If you would like to receive a free catalog featuring additional Hay House books and products, or if you would like information about the Hay Foundation, please contact:

Hay House, Inc.
P.O. Box 5100
Carlsbad, CA 92018-5100

(760) 431-7695 or **(800) 654-5126**
(760) 431-6948 (fax) or **(800) 650-5115 (fax)**
www.hayhouse.com

Published and distributed in Australia by:
Hay House Australia Pty. Ltd. • 18/36 Ralph St.
Alexandria NSW 2015 • *Phone:* 612-9669-4299
Fax: 612-9669-4144 • www.hayhouse.com.au

Published and distributed in the United Kingdom by:
Hay House UK, Ltd. • Unit 62, Canalot Studios
222 Kensal Rd., London W10 5BN
Phone: 44-20-8962-1230 • *Fax:* 44-20-8962-1239
www.hayhouse.co.uk

Published and distributed in the Republic of South Africa by:
Hay House SA (Pty), Ltd., P.O. Box 990, Witkoppen 2068
Phone/Fax: 27-11-706-6612 • orders@psdprom.co.za

Distributed in Canada by:
Raincoast • 9050 Shaughnessy St., Vancouver, B.C. V6P
6E5 • *Phone:* (604) 323-7100 • *Fax:* (604) 323-2600

Tune in to **www.hayhouseradio.com** for the best in inspirational talk radio featuring top Hay House authors! And, sign up via the Hay House USA Website to receive the Hay House online newsletter and stay informed about what's going on with your favorite authors. You'll receive bimonthly announcements about: Discounts and Offers, Special Events, Product Highlights, Free Excerpts, Giveaways, and more!
www.hayhouse.com

If you'd like to receive a catalog of Hay House books and products, or a free copy of one or more of our authors' newsletters, please visit **www.hayhouse.com**™ or detach and mail this reply card.

Tune in to Hay House Radio to listen to your favorite authors: **www.hayhouseradio.com**™

Yes, I'd like to receive:

☐ **a Hay House catalog**
☐ *The Christiane Northrup Newsletter*

☐ *The Louise Hay Newsletter*
☐ *The Sylvia Browne Newsletter*

Name _____

Address _____

City _____ State _____ Zip _____

E-mail _____

Also, please send:

To:

☐ **a Hay House catalog**
☐ *The Christiane Northrup Newsletter*

☐ *The Louise Hay Newsletter*
☐ *The Sylvia Browne Newsletter*

Name _____

Address _____

City _____ State _____ Zip _____

E-mail _____

To:

HAY HOUSE, INC.
P.O. Box 5100
Carlsbad, CA 92018-5100